there

WE FOUND OUR FAMILY IN A
NEW YORK CITY SUBWAY STATION

PETER MERCURIO

THERE
We Found Our Family In A New York City Subway Station

PETER MERCURIO

Copyright ©2025 by Peter Mercurio

All rights reserved.

No part of this publication may be reproduced, distributed, or transmitted in any form or by any means, including photocopying, recording, or other electronic or mechanical methods, without the prior written permission of the publisher, except as permitted by U.S. copyright law.

Some dialogue in this book is not intended to be a verbatim transcription; rather, it seeks to convey the feeling and meaning of the conversation. In every instance, the essence of the dialogue remains accurate. For privacy reasons, names and identifying characteristics for some people portrayed in this book have been changed.

Cover art courtesy of Matt Sauer.

ISBN: 979-8-9926373-2-8 (paperback)
ISBN: 979-8-9926373-9-7 (ebook)

for
Danny and Kevin

CONTENTS

MIRACLE

BEFORE FOREVER	3
BEYOND THE TURNSTILE	5
A MODEST HERO	13
TESTIMONY	20
NEEDS LOVE, MAKE PRETTY, APPLY TEMPLATE	30
LOST	34
PROS AND CONS	41
PRINCE AND THE PEA	48
A VIEW OF THE BRIDGE	59

FATE

NEW HOPE	70
GUARDIAN ANGEL	74
NO TIME LIKE THE PRESENT	82
PICKING UP BABY	89
FIRST NIGHT, SILENT NIGHT	95
SHINING STAR	103
NO RETURNS	111
CHILD CARE	116
CABIN FEVER	123
SOMETHING SPECIAL	131
FIRSTS	140
ONE STEP AHEAD, ONE STEP BACK	150
FAMILY	158

FOREVER

SKIN DEEP	164
WHERE THERE'S SMOKE	170
UNEXPECTED	174
HIS STORY	182
CURIOSITY	193
A DREAM	199
MAKING PROGRESS	202
PRE-CANA	210
THERE	225
ACKNOWLEDGMENTS	235
ABOUT THE AUTHOR	237
SNAPSHOTS	238

MIRACLE

*There are only two ways to live your life.
One is as though nothing is a miracle.
The other is as though everything is a miracle.*

Anonymous

BEFORE FOREVER

If he hadn't glanced back, we wouldn't be a family.

Monday, August 28, 2000

7:45pm

Danny was late.

He was supposed to leave work early, go to his apartment in Morningside Heights, pick up his accumulated mail, and then come to my place so we could go for dinner.

My stomach growled. Loud. Angry.

Danny missed exits and turns all the time. A dyslexic compass, he confused right for left and left for right and could walk a block or two in the wrong direction before snapping to and correcting course. It wouldn't be surprising if he were walking and whistling television theme songs—another of his unconscious reflexes. For sure a mash-up of his favorites: *The Andy Griffith Show*, *Bewitched*, and *Dallas*. That's my boyfriend: Opie, Samantha, and JR all rolled into one.

7:50pm

My roommate Joe laughed while watching a videotaped rerun of *Strangers With Candy*. I could've joined him in the living room like I had many times before, but I paced and waited instead.

Impatient.

The opposite of Danny. He had more patience than anyone I knew. If only I could absorb some of his.

From my bedroom window, nothing but noise. A bus screeched into the stop below and exhaled a hiss of fumes. The exhaust seeped into the room and up my nose. Taxis honked. A train roared underground, and the floor shook. It did that every other minute.

With a firehouse a few blocks north, St. Vincent's hospital a few blocks south, a bus stop below, and a major subway station underground, the cacophony never let up. Even though I had lived on the corner of 7th Avenue and 14th Street for six years, I was still not used to the overstimulation.

7:55pm

I wasn't really worried about him. Danny always showed up. Eventually.

I often joked that his chronic mental lapses were a result of his Southern upbringing. To that, he'd remind me, "Texas is not the South," with a pleasant, bless-your-heart tone that implied I was a silly, misinformed Yankee.

"Well, it is south of here," I'd say.

"Funny," he'd say, "I always seem to get where I need to be."

He was right about that. Although he rarely took the most direct route, Danny always managed to arrive at his destination. In fact, for all I knew, he was already there.

But there wasn't my apartment.

Then my phone rang.

BEYOND THE TURNSTILE

I picked up after one ring.
"I found a baby!" Danny shouted.
"What?" I asked, thinking I'd misheard.
"I found a baby!"
"Where are you?"
"I called 911, but no one's coming. I don't think they believed me, and I used my last quarter to call you. Can you call 911 and—"
"Wait. What? Where are you?" I asked.
"15th Street and 8th Avenue."
"I'm coming down."
I had never heard Danny sound so frantic. By nature, he's remarkably calm and centered. His pulse, quiet and steady. But that night, I could feel his heart pounding through the phone.
"Danny found a baby." I ran into the living room.
"What?" Joe asked.
"Danny found a baby. You wanna come?"
"No," he said, pointing to the television. "I'm good."

The door slammed behind me. As I sprinted down the stairs and across Fifteenth Street, I felt a force propelling me across traffic, around pedestrians, dogs, and garbage piles.

I found a baby.

Danny's panicked words echoed in my head.

Then all I heard were my huffs.

A police car's lights flashed in the distance outside the A/C/E subway exit. Looking pale, shocked, and confused, Danny stood alone at the top of the steps.

"Where's the baby?" I asked, out of breath. Danny answered with a tilt of his head. Just then, the baby, wrapped in a black sweatshirt and cradled in a policeman's arms, ascended from below.

A chill pulsed up my spine. The policeman and the bundled baby stopped directly in front of us. I could only see a tiny area of the baby's head. The flashing hues of red and blue wiped across our faces, disorienting and bending reality. I strained my neck to get a better look. The baby yawned. I wanted to stroke his forehead or caress his plump brown cheeks, an impulse to touch and help soothe this little miracle stretching his jaw in front of us. I resisted the urge.

But I wondered if Danny had touched him. And then more questions flooded my mind. Where exactly did he find him? On the platform? In a trash can? How did he find him? But with my heart in my throat, the words didn't come. Danny reached out and took my hand in his. Our fingers meshed and tangled as one.

More cops and a slew of detectives in tweed jackets seemed to materialize out of thin air, arriving from all directions. The scene looked like just another *Law & Order* shoot that regularly took place in our neighborhood.

"Stay put," a detective told Danny. We waited and stared at the baby. The authorities scoured the area for evidence.

Unimpressed by the commotion around him, the baby yawned again—without a peep.

A million thoughts raced through my head. Who could leave a baby like this? And why? None of it seemed real. Not Danny, not the policeman, not even the baby.

Garbled static from police radios broke in and out. The staccato snapped me back to reality. Where was the ambulance? St. Vincent's was just a few blocks away. The baby could have been brought there and back on foot several times by now. What was taking so long?

A passerby stopped next to us and asked, "What happened?"

"Somebody left a baby," I replied.

"Oh my god," she said. "How could someone do something like this?" She glanced at the baby. "Look how adorable."

"He found the baby," I said, pointing to Danny.

"You found him?"

"Yes," Danny said.

"If I were you, I would have taken him home with me," she said with a loopy chuckle. "You saved a life. You're a hero." She patted Danny's arm, took one final look at the baby, then muttered "God bless" before walking away.

Another police car pulled up. "We'll transport to St. Vincent's ourselves," a nearby officer said into his radio.

"Roger that," a voice on the other end pierced the static. The officer with the baby got in the car and closed the door. And just like that, the baby, who had been within arm's reach a second earlier, was gone.

"You know you're going to be connected to that kid for the rest of your life, don't you?" I whispered as we watched the car drive away.

"How?" Danny asked.

"I don't know. Maybe not tomorrow or next year, but in the future. When he learns about this night and how he was saved, he'll want to meet the person who found him."

We stood close, still holding hands, as two officers cordoned off the subway exit with yellow tape that warned "POLICE LINE. DO NOT CROSS." Garbage bins for Doherty's, a greasy spoon diner on the corner, reeked of decaying food. We leaned against the brick wall, trying to stay out of the way of both the detectives and the smell.

"Don't go anywhere," an officer reminded Danny.

For the next hour, several detectives and police officers questioned Danny. They were terse and remarkably indifferent, given the circumstances. Individually, in pairs, and at random intervals, they asked Danny the same questions. Each time, he calmly recounted how he found the baby. Some interviewers took notes, while others just listened attentively to his answers. Since I stood nearby, one of the officers asked who I was and why I was there. I gestured to Danny and explained that we were boyfriends and he had called me for help. The officer asked where I lived. I answered, and he nodded slowly before turning away.

"Don't look now," I said, "but there's a news van to your left." Danny looked to the right. "Your other left."

A reporter from WPIX-TV and one from the *New York Daily News* clamored for an interview. Danny agreed to speak with them. The *Daily News* reporter went first. I stood as close as possible to listen in. As the interviews unfolded, a clearer picture developed:

- He saw a doll under a blanket.
- The legs moved.
- His heart stopped. (Danny's, not the baby's.)
- He called 911, then me.
- The baby was docile.

The TV news reporter stood by for his turn. Once again, Danny repeated the story for the fifth or sixth time. That interview finished a few minutes before 10 pm.

My stomach growled, and I suddenly realized that Danny, still in shock, needed to eat.

The WPIX reporter stepped in front of the camera, reviewed his notes, and prepared for a live lead to the 10 o'clock news. We were going to miss it. From the same pay phone Danny had used earlier, I called Joe to ask him to record the 10 o'clock news on Channel 11.

The temperature, unseasonably cool and breezy for August, ruled out a sidewalk café. Instead, Danny and I walked a block to Maryann's, a Mexican restaurant, and promptly ordered margaritas. The place would've been bustling earlier in the night, but at 10 pm on a late summer Monday, it was quiet and empty, except for the staff and a few others finishing their meals.

Danny and I sat in silence for a few minutes, unable to articulate what had just happened. When we finally spoke, all that came out was, "Wow." But mostly, we sat in stunned disbelief until our drinks arrived.

"You know," Danny broke the silence, then sipped his drink, "I had just missed getting on a train at 110th Street. If I made that train…" He trailed off, momentarily lost in thought. "Wow, a few seconds earlier and…"

I wanted him to finish his thought. No. I wanted him to start from the beginning. But Danny, no longer fueled by adrenaline, seemed shaken. Tears welled up in his eyes—a rare display of emotion that surprised me.

"Are you okay?" I asked.

"How can someone just leave a newborn baby like that? An infant."

"I know." I reached out and held his hand. "I still don't know all the details, exactly how you found him."

Danny shot me a curious look as if I had been with him the entire time, and then he began to fill in the gaps.

"I was exiting the station, and as I pushed through the turnstile, I noticed something on the ground to my left, behind the bars in the corner. It looked like the legs of a doll sticking out of a black hoodie. I wondered why someone would leave a doll there. It looked so life-like. I kept going, and about halfway up the stairs, I glanced back. And that's when the legs moved. My heart pounded. I jumped back down. When I got close, I realized it wasn't a doll but a real baby. My mind started racing. This can't be real. Is this a setup for some hidden camera show? I thought, 'Am I being watched? Is this a test?' All those thoughts happened in a nanosecond. I wasn't going to take a chance it was a joke. I needed to get help. But I couldn't get back into the station. I was on the outside of an exit-only. I banged on the bars and called out to get someone's attention. People just kept on walking past me. I yelled for them to alert the token booth worker. No one stopped. One woman came closer but didn't speak English and couldn't understand what I was saying—even after I pointed to the baby and begged her to get help. I probably looked like a crazy person. I didn't know what to do. I mean, I didn't want to pick the baby up because… what if he was injured and I caused more harm? Also, I figured the authorities would treat the area as a crime scene, and I didn't want to disturb any evidence. But I needed help. So I raced up the steps to the pay phone on the corner to call 911. After I told them my location, I went back to wait with the baby. I stroked his head and said, 'It'll be okay,' but he started to whimper and cry, so I stopped. I loosened the sweatshirt around his… Part of the umbilical cord was still attached. Covered in petroleum jelly."

Danny's face glazed over. Overwhelmed, he disappeared into his thoughts for a moment.

"I'm sure it was only a few minutes, but it seemed it was taking too long for help to arrive. I thought maybe the 911 operator didn't believe me. So I called you. I figured you could flag down a cop on the street while I stayed with the baby. Luckily, I had another quarter on me. But the police had arrived right after we hung up."

"Maybe this is the universe telling us we should get cell phones." I tried to lighten the mood.

"Don't think it works like that," he smiled for the first time that night.

"Yeah, we don't need them." I nodded and smiled back.

The drinks and food took the edge off. We decompressed and even joked about how incredible it was that typically unobservant Danny was the one person out of eight million people in New York City to discover an abandoned baby. And with tequila in our system, the whole night started to take on the aura of a tall tale, like a fisherman bragging about the catch that got away.

But except for a stroke of coincidence, timing, and awareness, Danny somehow noticed a "doll" in a black hoodie tucked away in a dark, secluded corner of a subway station. This sight, so out of the ordinary, captured his attention just long enough to give him a moment's pause. That fateful glance back was nothing short of a miracle.

On our walk home, we passed by the subway station. Other than a pulled patch of police tape snagged on a bolt, it appeared as if nothing had happened. We stopped at the top of the steps and peered down. There was no need for words. The shocking truth hit us with a sobering force: a newborn baby had been abandoned here.

"What if his legs didn't move and I kept going?" Danny asked. "Then what?" His voice, soft and solemn, cracked. "What if nobody else saw him?"

I had no answer to offer. We said little else for the rest of the walk home.

Joe was still up when we arrived. He leapt off the futon and hugged Danny. "Oh my god," he said, "I can't believe it." Joe pointed at the television to a cued-up and paused still frame of Danny, his mouth agape, suspended in mid-sentence. "You look great on the news," Joe added. He rewound the tape. "But you have to see it from the beginning. Breaking news, the lead story."

We watched the report multiple times. Since Joe had already seen it, he kept one eye on the TV and the other on Danny, relishing his reactions.

Naturally, Joe had questions. Heck, I still had some. And Danny, who was fading, answered as many as he could. The three of us speculated on who and why someone would abandon a baby there, in one of the gayest neighborhoods in the city, if not the world.

All talked out, we called it a night around 1 am, and Danny and I made our way to the bedroom. Our clothes and the evening melted to the floor. We crawled under the covers and curled up. Danny was fast asleep as soon as his head hit the pillow.

But my mind refused to turn off, consumed by thoughts of tragic worst-case scenarios. I imagined what might have transpired if Danny had been on time. What if he had been one step quicker and caught the earlier train? What if he hadn't found the baby? How would our night have unfolded if he hadn't glanced back? Like nothing had happened: We meet for dinner. We make small talk about our days, return home, brush our teeth, climb into bed, switch on the local news, and see a story about an abandoned baby, possibly dead, at a nearby subway station. We shake our heads, comment about how sad it is, and ask ourselves, "What's wrong with this world?" Then we turn out the lights and fall asleep. Both of us. Easily.

But Danny was late. He glanced back. He saw the tiny legs poking out. And he didn't walk by. The baby was alive. The baby was breathing. Danny didn't uncover a tragedy. He uncovered a miracle. And though we were unaware at the time, he had forever altered the path of our lives.

A MODEST HERO

Around 6 am the next morning, the phone rang. Thinking it had to be important, I answered, groggy and slightly hungover. On the other end was the guy temporarily subletting Danny's apartment, and he wasn't pleased. I handed the phone to Danny. He listened and then apologized several times before hanging up.

"What was that about?" I asked.

"He said my phone rang nonstop all night, and he couldn't figure out how to silence it, so he pulled the line out of the wall. When he plugged the cord back in this morning, the phone rang again a second later. He wanted me to know about all the calls."

"Why didn't you tell him what happened last night?"

"I'm hardly awake. I didn't want to get into it."

Danny sat up in bed and called to retrieve his messages. One side of his face displayed a crisscrossed pattern, branded from a motionless night sleeping on my creased T-shirt sleeve. I turned on the halogen lamp and adjusted the dimmer to low. My left shoulder was chafed with clustered prick marks from

Danny's coarse stubble. Some mornings it looked like I had slept on a bed of nails. I wiggled my jaw and massaged my shoulder.

Danny listened to over a dozen messages. All the local television news stations wanted in-person, on-camera interviews with the hero who saved the baby. One by one, he listened and announced the network. "That was CBS." I held out a pad and a pen, but he waved me off. "NBC… ABC… Fox… New York One… Univision." Some reporters and producers left multiple messages. Danny said he'd listen to them at work and return the calls from there.

That morning, like every other, Joe woke up before us. He usually left for work before 8 am. Danny and I started work at 10 am. We rarely saw Joe in the morning, and given that we had one bathroom the size of a broom closet, that was a good thing. But Joe had left and come back. A copy of the *Daily News* sat on the dining table, opened to the headline, "Straphanger Saves Infant: New Yorkers to the Rescue." Accompanying the article was a large, stunning photo of Danny gesturing down the subway steps. He looked like a bold, life-saving superhero. A fantasy figure. And as a social worker, it wasn't too far from the truth. In much more subtle ways, he helped save lives every day.

Danny subleased his apartment and "moved in" with Joe and me so all three of us could save money. Rent split three ways was better than two. The three of us got along great. We often ate dinner, watched movies, played games, or had friends over to do all of the above. Sure, it was a tight squeeze in a 400-square-foot converted one-bedroom, but we rarely got on each other's nerves because we enjoyed each other's company. We respected each other's privacy as much as we could. Of course, with only a partition separating Joe from the rest of the living room, his privacy was compromised more than ours. We could at least close our bedroom door.

As a bonus, Danny and I could walk to our jobs together. He worked as a clinical caseworker and a volunteer support group facilitator at Gay Men's Health Crisis (GMHC), while I worked part-time as a word processor and presentation designer for a medical advertising agency. Our route took us past a food cart, where we often stopped for a muffin and coffee. However, I called in sick the day after Danny found the baby. After what had happened, my job seemed even more soulless than usual. Unlike me, Danny defined "sick day" strictly as being too physically ill to work.

Before leaving, Danny searched for his keys. He often misplaced them, and there was always an air of suspense about where they might be. He yanked yesterday's pants from the hamper and checked the pockets.

"Found 'em," he said, then headed for the door.

I straightened his collar, placed both hands on his shoulders, and reminded him to keep breathing. "Let me know how the calls go," I said, giving him a quick peck goodbye.

When Danny got outside, he started walking north towards work but stopped. He turned around and looked down the block at St. Vincent's Hospital. Going there hadn't been his plan, but the baby was on his mind, and he wanted to know how the baby was doing. So he decided to head to St. Vincent's.

At the information desk, he asked to see the abandoned baby brought in the night before.

"Are you family?" the woman at the desk asked officiously.

"No. I'm the person who found him," he said.

"I'm sorry, only family," she said politely but curtly, ending the conversation.

"But he has no family."

She shook her head, and Danny was unable to see the baby.

At work, Danny found it impossible to concentrate. Not only was his mind preoccupied, but his coworkers, excited from seeing him on the news and in the paper, kept stopping by his cubicle to hear his firsthand account. A few even joked, "Why didn't you just take him home?"

Danny glanced at the list of unanswered telephone messages. Feeling overwhelmed with the idea of giving interviews, he sought advice from GMHC's media director on handling the requests. He decided only to do interviews that felt right and could accommodate his work schedule. Then, one by one, he began returning the calls.

He scheduled some interviews during his lunch break and the rest for after work. Off camera, one reporter asked how he remained so calm. Danny explained that his experience and training in dealing with crisis situations must have somehow prepared him. Little did the reporter know that Danny hadn't yet processed his emotions. Making sense of it all would come later.

For the rest of the day, Danny had difficulty focusing on anything other than the baby. A coworker suggested calling the hospital's pediatric social worker to learn more, so Danny called the hospital between the interviews.

After several unsuccessful attempts, someone finally answered the call. Danny introduced himself and inquired about the baby's well-being.

"How did you get this number?" the woman on the other end asked.

"I'm the person who found the baby," he replied.

She paused momentarily, then calmly explained that privacy laws prevented her from sharing information. He had figured as much—and understood. His job required strict adherence to confidentiality protocols.

"Is the baby okay?" he asked, hoping she would ease his mind. Besides, he couldn't see how revealing the baby's condition would violate confidentiality laws.

"He's healthy and in excellent condition," she said. "But I can't tell you much more than that."

Danny made a final plea to see the baby, but the social worker remained unwavering. The conversation left him with mixed emotions—relief and disappointment. He called me to share his thwarted visit and unfruitful conversation.

"I'll see if Nick knows anything," I said. Nick, our friend and a doctor associated with St. Vincent's, was the only person we could think of who might have access to more information. I left him a detailed message. Nick called back a few hours later. He had asked around and learned that a biological relative, the baby's grandmother, had come forward to claim the child.

When I relayed the news to Danny, he seemed relieved. He envisioned a doting grandmother who would raise the boy with love. I was less optimistic. In my opinion, a woman who raised a daughter to abandon her baby hadn't done a good enough job the first time. Danny's faith in humanity far surpasses my own.

Throughout the day and evening, I anxiously awaited news reports, switching between stations to avoid missing any. I loaded blank videocassettes into our VCR and Joe's to record every one of Danny's appearances.

That evening, Danny, Joe, and I watched all the recorded footage. We had a media darling and superstar in our midst. Joe and I couldn't help teasing Danny for giving almost identical answers in each interview. Regardless of the interviewer or network, some variation of "he was docile" or "the baby was docile" made it into every report. Depending on the station, either "Good Samaritan," "Hero," or "Found Baby" appeared beneath Danny's name.

"Why do they have to put 'hero' under my name?" he asked.

"Because you are," Joe said.

"Anyone passing by would have done the same thing."

"But they didn't. You did. So shut up about it. You're a hero." Joe cut right to the heart of the matter, leaving no room for argument.

After the day's media frenzy, we thought Danny's fifteen minutes of fame had ended. However, a local CBS reporter requested a follow-up interview the following day. Danny scheduled it for after work. For fun, Joe and I showed up and played extras in the background on the sidewalk. No matter what we did, we couldn't upstage the superhero.

The follow-up interview led off the local CBS news at 11 pm the next night, and it tugged at our emotions. Rather than simply recapping the events, the reporter focused on the emotional aspect of the story, particularly Danny's serendipitous glance back at the baby at the exact moment his legs wiggled.

"This is the story of Daniel Stewart, listening to that little voice inside all of us," the reporter said. "A good detective listens to theirs. And sometimes acting on that little voice takes a little nudging."

A nanosecond of stillness, Danny goes on his way without a second thought. We watched the report again and again, feeling chills each time. When it ended, I hit rewind. We listened to the tape whir, watched Danny's face distort in reverse, and played it again from the beginning.

However, Danny's media appearances were not finished. There were a few more to fulfill in the coming days.

A producer from *Montel* contacted him. They were planning a show about abandoned babies and safe haven laws, which New York had recently implemented. The producer informed Danny that Montel Williams had seen the news and wanted him as a guest on the show. Danny felt hesitant. Some talk shows thrived on controversy, and he had no desire to exploit the situation or get caught up in any drama solely for the sake of ratings. The producer assured him that would not happen. Montel simply wished for him to share his story.

Danny agreed, and a day or two later, he found himself in the studio for the taping. The producer briefed him on the schedule and prepared him for what to expect. Soon, he was escorted onto the set, and before he knew it, Montel introduced him to the audience as the man who had found a baby on the subway. "We have that man here with us today," he said, "Please welcome Danny Stewart."

And then, in what Danny described as a whirlwind blur, he recounted the story for the umpteenth time.

Afterward, Montel addressed the audience, saying, "This man is a hero."

Danny smiled but felt a slight cringe from this label.

But Montel wasn't finished with the praise.

"You saved a life," he said. "You're a very rare person. A lot of people probably saw that little bundle lying there the other night and they walked by, and they kept walking because they didn't want to get involved. They didn't want to be the person that had to make a decision about what to do with that baby. I thank you. I know you'd probably do that for somebody else that was hurting. That's the kind of person you are."

The hero label had stuck.

Danny would simply have to grin and accept it.

TESTIMONY

After his appearance on *Montel*, the curtain finally fell on Danny's fifteen minutes of fame. We resumed our ordinary, everyday lives, although they were anything but ordinary or routine in the autumn of 2000. Rehearsals for my play, *Yesterday's News*, began right after Labor Day. As the producer and director, I was consumed with the show. Danny helped with production tasks as much as he could. When the show opened in October, Danny and Joe ran the box office. This coincided with the final push for my sister Linda's campaign for the U.S. House of Representatives in the Fifth Congressional District of New Jersey.

Earlier that year, Linda had asked me to be her full-time Campaign Manager, but I declined. My focus was on building Other Side Productions, the nonprofit theater company I had recently founded. She begged, and I eventually agreed to be her Senior Advisor and Primary Confidant. This role soon expanded to Chief Strategist, Volunteer Coordinator, Graphic Designer, and Web Master.

Throughout the fall, Danny and I spent every waking second at our day jobs, the theater, or in New Jersey's Fifth Congressional district canvassing and promoting Linda's campaign. We knocked on doors, handed out brochures, and hung posters on roadside telephone poles, mainly at night.

Back in the city, we scoured the sidewalks for discarded televisions. In line with the play's theme of a ubiquitous news media's corruption of innocence, I had envisioned television sets covering the entire stage, serving as tables, chairs, and other set pieces. In less than a week, Danny had gone from a hero rescuing an abandoned baby to a stagehand salvaging abandoned televisions. We brought the TVs back to our apartment and stacked them from floor to ceiling in our bedroom and part of the living room until we could load them into the theatre.

With both the campaign and production consuming our energy, along with the excitement of the once-in-a-lifetime Mets-Yankees Subway Series, Danny and I rarely discussed the baby. Occasionally, Danny shared the story of how he found the baby with someone new, but for the most part, we were too preoccupied to think much about the baby's current situation. However, one day in mid-October, two months after Danny found the baby, Karen Navarro, an attorney from the Administration for Children's Services (ACS), called him unexpectedly.

"The police report only had your name and no other contact information," Karen explained. "So I started calling every Daniel Stewart in the white pages until I found you."

As the prosecuting attorney for ACS, part of Karen's job was to prove the baby's abandonment in order to terminate the biological parent's rights and consequently free the baby for adoption. Although she could have relied solely on the police report and corroborating evidence, she wanted to strengthen her case with Danny's eyewitness testimony. Since he was the only eyewitness, his testimony would help move the process forward.

Danny didn't fully understand all the legalities and why Karen needed him to testify. After all, hadn't a grandmother come forward? But he didn't ask her about that. If his testimony could help the baby in any way, he would do whatever Karen asked. In the end, it wasn't his choice to make anyway. Karen issued a formal subpoena commanding him to appear on October 23rd.

During their conversation, Danny inquired about the baby.

"He's doing fine," Karen said. "Did you know he has your name?"

"My name?" Danny said, confused.

"Yes," she said, "His name is Daniel Ace Doe."

Taken aback, Danny couldn't speak.

"Nurses at the hospital chose Daniel after you," Karen continued, "and the police chose Ace after the subway line where you found him."

The fact that people he didn't know and had never met named the baby after him caught Danny by surprise. Emotions rarely got the best of him, but twice now, circumstances involving this baby, Daniel Ace, had stirred an ache in his soul.

"What an honor," he said.

In the two weeks preceding Danny's court appearance, we never discussed the trial, his testimony, or the baby. We were swamped with work and barely got our clothes off at the end of the day before crashing on the bed.

On the morning of the 23rd, Danny was eager, a little nervous, but mostly excited about going to family court.

"I wonder if my namesake will be there," he said before leaving.

Karen met him in the courtroom waiting area. She introduced herself and then told him about a last-minute change of plans. All the necessary paperwork wasn't in order, and the trial had to be postponed.

A week later, Danny received another subpoena commanding him to appear on December 4th. By then, with my show closed and Linda's campaign over, our lives would be less hectic..

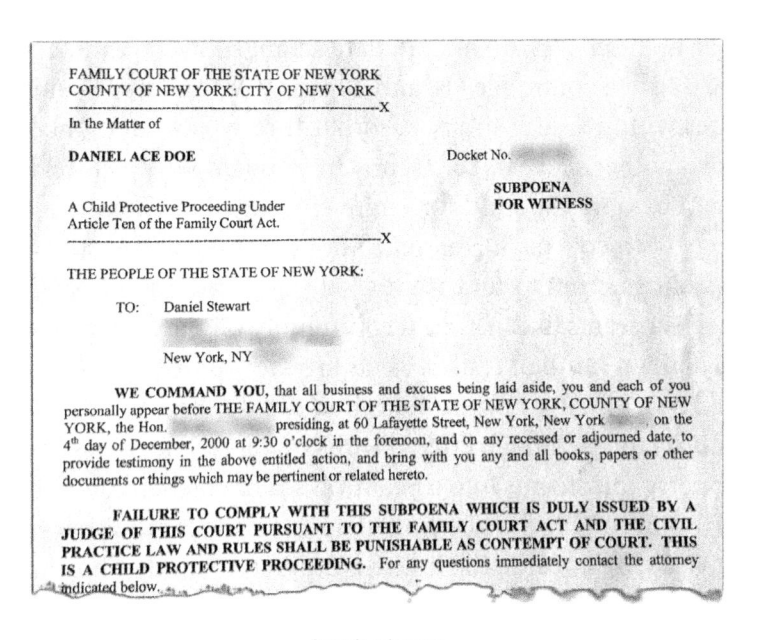

```
FAMILY COURT OF THE STATE OF NEW YORK
COUNTY OF NEW YORK: CITY OF NEW YORK
-------------------------------------------------X
In the Matter of

DANIEL ACE DOE                              Docket No.

                                                SUBPOENA
A Child Protective Proceeding Under             FOR WITNESS
Article Ten of the Family Court Act.
-------------------------------------------------X

THE PEOPLE OF THE STATE OF NEW YORK:

     TO:   Daniel Stewart

           New York, NY

     WE COMMAND YOU, that all business and excuses being laid aside, you and each of you personally appear before THE FAMILY COURT OF THE STATE OF NEW YORK, COUNTY OF NEW YORK, the Hon.            presiding, at 60 Lafayette Street, New York, New York      on the 4th day of December, 2000 at 9:30 o'clock in the forenoon, and on any recessed or adjourned date, to provide testimony in the above entitled action, and bring with you any and all books, papers or other documents or things which may be pertinent or related hereto.

     FAILURE TO COMPLY WITH THIS SUBPOENA WHICH IS DULY ISSUED BY A JUDGE OF THIS COURT PURSUANT TO THE FAMILY COURT ACT AND THE CIVIL PRACTICE LAW AND RULES SHALL BE PUNISHABLE AS CONTEMPT OF COURT. THIS IS A CHILD PROTECTIVE PROCEEDING. For any questions immediately contact the attorney indicated below.
```

Danny's subpoena

Danny and I spent Thanksgiving apart that year. He flew to Texas to be with his family while I drove across the Hudson to be with mine.

Our families, although different in many ways, shared certain similarities. My parents, born seven months apart in 1940, met while attending City College of New York. They were the first in their families to earn a college degree. After graduation, they married and had my brother Joe 9 months later. Linda arrived eighteen months after that. Between Linda and me, they had another baby who unfortunately didn't survive childbirth. I came along smack-dab in the middle of 1968, which some historians consider one of the worst years in modern American history. All five of us lived in a small one-bedroom apartment in Greenpoint until my younger brother

Matthew was born a year later. Then we moved to a small three-bedroom house on a quarter acre in Westwood, New Jersey.

Danny's parents were born two years apart—his dad in 1935 and his mom in 1937. They met at a football game between their high schools, on a blind date arranged by a friend. They married at a young age (18 and 20 years old) and had Danny's sister within a year and his brother three years later. Then it took another six years for Danny to come into the picture. He was the youngest child for eighteen years, but when Danny went off to college, his parents adopted three more children, all siblings, from foster care.

His parents live in a rural community on the outskirts of a small town south of Dallas. Their fifty-acre property is mainly used as a grazing pasture for a horse, a donkey, and about a dozen cattle. Although littered with cow patty land mines, their property transforms into a beautiful sea of bluebonnets in the spring. At night, the howling of coyotes pierces the peaceful star-filled sky. Inside the house is a different kind of howling: Christian evangelists preaching the Bible through all the intercom speakers. Danny's mom, a devout Southern Baptist and fundamentalist, filled her home with the good word.

On the other hand, my devout Roman Catholic mom filled her home with a different kind of gospel: the scents of sauces and confections. A house without food, especially one that didn't smell like garlic or cake, wasn't a home. And she would recite the contents of the refrigerator as soon as you walked in. *Are you hungry? We've got plenty to eat. There's eggplant parm. I made escarole soup. You want soup?* My dad would always chime in with a testimonial: *The soup is delicious. I had it earlier over some noodles.* Before you knew it, all the plastic containers and foil-wrapped leftovers would be lined up on the counter, waiting for you to "make a plate," even if you weren't hungry.

As for our fathers, in contrast to my dad's gregarious style, Danny's dad is a reserved man of few words. When he does speak, it's with a thick, mumbled drawl that begs for subtitles, although I remember this one time he spoke as clearly as day.

Danny and I were having dinner with his folks at a barbecue joint in Texas. While chewing on beef brisket, his dad referred to one of his cattle, a calf, by saying, "That one there will make good hamburger." No subtitles were necessary.

In contrast, dead air makes my dad uncomfortable. If he's not talking, he's not breathing. So he fills silence with hot air, mostly his own.

Both of our parents started their lives with very little. But they worked hard, saved, and carved out a middle-class existence for themselves and their children. Our dads woke up early and worked long days. Our moms did the same, both inside and outside the home. They loved their families and sacrificed so their kids would have better lives. While our respective family upbringings were culturally and stylistically different, they were also alike in one significant way: both Texans and New Yorkers think they are the center of the universe.

When Danny returned from his Texan Thanksgiving in 2000, another big meal awaited him. My mom had prepared a second Thanksgiving dinner—not leftovers—just for him (and us, too). She felt bad Danny hadn't been with us, but in reality, she was looking for any excuse to cook, eat, and bring the family together.

The conversation around the Thanksgiving II table included Danny's trip, the baby, a postmortem for Linda's campaign loss, my show's closure, and the unresolved presidential election. While we inhaled the feast, now complemented by Sunday macaronis and gravy, we exhaled sighs of relief that the nonstop whirlwind of that autumn was finally over.

But the breather would be short-lived.

December 4, 2000

Danny left the apartment early to get to the courthouse by 9:30 am. He hoped it wouldn't be another false alarm. He needed the trial to start on time. After six years at GMHC, he was leaving for a new job, and his exit interview was scheduled for later that morning. When he saw Karen in the waiting area, he told her about his time constraints. She assured him the trial would take less than ten to fifteen minutes.

Two other women—Terri, the baby's attorney from the Legal Aid Society, and Gail, a supervisor from Talbot Perkins Children's Services, the foster care agency of record—met them in the waiting area. Looking around, Danny noticed many unhappy faces—mothers, fathers, and children in domestic disputes or those caught up in the system.

Karen, Terri, and Gail briefed Danny about how the trial would proceed and what he could expect. They warned him about the judge. Each feared the judge's quick temper, especially when things weren't done to her satisfaction.

According to them, Judge Cooper demanded and expected efficiency, thoroughness, and competence, and if she didn't get it, watch out. Danny wondered what kind of wolf he was being fed to.

A clerk shouted the case number, and the women gathered their belongings to escort Danny into the courtroom. The judge watched their entrance as Gail motioned for Danny to sit behind a table directly across from the bench.

Glancing at Judge Cooper, Danny realized she didn't resemble the viper she was made out to be. Her diminutive frame suggested she wasn't someone to fear; instead, she looked like a fairy godmother about to share wisdom from on high.

The women briefed the judge on Baby Daniel Ace Doe's status. While the mention of the baby's name tugged at Danny's heartstrings, the matters before his testimony were purely procedural and dispassionate. Judge Cooper had seen and heard it all and couldn't waste time on extraneous emotions. After the women updated the judge, Karen called Danny to the witness stand.

Following instructions, Danny stated his name and swore to tell the truth. Although he was there to share his story rather than being on trial, the formality of the swearing-in racked his nerves. Judge Cooper looked him in the eye and let a grin slip out, causing her demeanor to instantly shift from stern to sweet.

"I'm delighted you're here," she said.

Whether for his benefit or not, she revealed herself as merely a sheep in wolf's clothing. Judge Cooper asked him to tell the court what happened on August 28th. By then, recounting the story had become second nature to Danny.

All eyes in the courtroom focused on Danny, causing him to momentarily lose his train of thought. He regained his composure and took a deep breath before telling his story.

Judge Cooper listened intently.

When Danny finished, she expressed her gratitude for saving the baby's life. Then she asked if he could stay for the remainder of the trial. Danny glanced at his watch, concerned about missing his exit interview.

"How long will it take?" he asked.

"Not long," the judge assured him.

Danny nodded and returned to his seat.

Karen called a detective to the stand, who quickly explained what happened that night in less than five minutes.

"Mr. Stewart," the judge turned to Danny, "let me explain what's going on here, the purpose of this trial. In cases of abandonment like this one, our goal is to place the child in a pre-adoptive foster home as quickly as possible." She explained that without any existing biological attachments, expediting the process was in the baby's best interest, as well as the court's and the city's.

No biological attachments? What about the grandmother who had come forward? Something didn't make sense to Danny. Why hadn't Gail, Karen, or Terri mentioned a grandmother in their updates? The absence of a biological family connection could only mean one thing: our friend Nicholas had been misinformed. No one had stepped forward to claim the baby.

Judge Cooper leaned over the bench, inching closer to Danny.

"Mr. Stewart, are you interested in adopting this baby?" She asked so matter-of-factly and softly that Danny was unsure if he had heard her correctly. He didn't say anything. He looked down to find or gather a response, then back up at the judge. Time stopped. He felt every eye in the room on him, waiting for his answer.

As a social worker, Danny knew the process of adopting a foster child could be arduous. And he had never heard of a judge giving a baby to someone she had just met a minute ago. Images of a new life flashed in his mind during those few seconds of reflection.

He took a deep breath, calmed his nerves, and finally responded.

"Yes, but I know it's not that easy," he said. The word "yes" slipped out before he could fully appreciate its meaning and implications.

"Well, it can be," the judge said.

Danny could only nod. Judge Cooper nodded back. Then she began issuing orders in rapid succession to Gail, Karen, and Terri:

1. Start a home study.
2. Arrange a visit with the baby.
3. Expedite all the necessary paperwork.

"Mr. Stewart," the judge said, "if you are serious about adopting this baby, you must appear at the next hearing."

Speechless, Danny nodded again.

Judge Cooper smiled and then glanced at her calendar. "Are you available in two weeks?"

Without checking, Danny said yes again.

"Good. Let's see…" Judge Cooper scanned her calendar. "How about Wednesday, December 20th at 9:30 am?"

"Okay," he said.

"Wonderful. I'll see you then. See how easy that was." The judge adjourned the trial and excused everyone from the courtroom.

"I've never seen anything like that before," Gail leaned over and whispered into Danny's ear. Neither had Karen or Terri.

Once back in the waiting area, Danny turned to the women and asked, "What just happened?"

Judge Cooper had just given them a lot to accomplish in little time. The three women began developing a plan for the next steps in the process, which now included Danny and, by extension, me. I just didn't know it yet.

Now late for his exit interview, Danny left the family court building and ran to the subway station.

NEEDS LOVE, MAKE PRETTY, APPLY TEMPLATE

"You're never going to believe this," Danny cut me off before I could say hello.

"Believe what?" I asked.

"The judge and the baby," he said, his voice cracking. "She asked if I was interested in adopting the baby."

"Are you kidding?"

"I'm not," he said, his voice rising above the rumble of the train as it pulled into the station.

"And what did you tell her?"

"I said 'yes.'"

"What? No. Go back there right now and tell her no." My gut, now in my throat, did the talking.

"I can't. My train's here." The brakes screeched in the background. "I gotta go. I'll call you when I get to work."

"Wait!"

He didn't respond.

Delivering breathtaking news from subway payphones was becoming a habit of his, like a modern-day Clark Kent. But instead of changing into Superman, Danny used payphones to give me heart attacks.

Above the cubicle dividers, I saw my coworkers' heads turned towards me. I put the receiver on the base, kept my hand on top, and stared at the Venn diagram on my monitor. I couldn't concentrate. The hand-drawn slide titled "A Paradigm Shift," or some other corporate-speak nonsense, with an account exec's scribbled instructions of "needs love, make pretty, apply template," would have to wait. I was in no shape to make anything pretty, especially not three overlapping ovals.

Was he serious?

I beelined to Maya's cubicle. She was a copy editor at the agency and a trusted friend who had flawlessly stage-managed both of my plays earlier that year. I needed her cues now more than ever. I took small, quick steps, moving like an expectant father I wasn't sure I wanted to be.

I peeked over her cubicle divider. An empty chair. I searched the kitchen. Not there either. I kept looking. When I heard her voice coming from Jim's office, I stopped and peeked inside.

A creative team huddled over a project timeline. I tapped the door with my elbow. It opened a bit. I pushed harder and stood in the doorway, waiting for someone to notice. As sharp as ever, Maya saw me immediately and squinted, studying my expressionless face with one eye.

"Are you all right?" she asked. "You look like you've seen a ghost."

"I'm sorry to interrupt," I said. "But I…"

"What's wrong?" Jim asked.

"Um…"

If I had thought it through beforehand, I could have asked Maya to step outside. But now I had an audience: an account executive, an art director, a copywriter, an editor, a project coordinator, and a guy from production.

I couldn't contain it any longer.

"I just got off the phone with Danny. A judge asked him to adopt the baby he found last August." I blurted out the words in one breath, then surveyed their mostly slack-jawed faces. Some furrowed their brows, unsure if this was a prank. It was understandable since I had a reputation for office mischief—hiding staplers, unplugging phone wires, and indiscriminately lobbing crumpled paper grenades over the cubicles.

"Wow," Jim broke the silence, "that's amazing."

His words prompted others to join the conversation.

"Unbelievable."

"So beautiful."

"Incredible."

"Wait!" Maya removed her glasses and let them hang around her neck. "You can't just drop a bomb like that and not expect us to have questions."

"I just got a call from Danny outside family court," I explained. "That's all I know."

Maya stood up and put her arm around my shoulder.

"I don't think I can do this," I said.

A chorus of "Yes, you can" echoed in response.

"You have to do this," Maya squeezed my shoulder.

"I can babysit," the copywriter offered.

"Me too," said the art director.

"Me three," someone else chimed in. Instant babysitters for a hypothetical baby.

I tensed up. Didn't they realize Danny and I were in no position to become dads?

My part-time status at the ad agency was by design. My design. This survival job allowed me to pursue ambitions outside the office. I barely earned enough to support myself—how would I provide for a kid?

Feeling guilty for not sharing my coworkers' excitement, I retreated to my cubicle.

The voicemail indicator blinked. It was a message from Danny. "Hey, it's me. Where are you? I only have a minute before my exit interview. Then I have client and staff meetings the rest of the day. All right. Don't bother calling me back. We'll catch up later at home," he concluded with an unmistakable and perky twinkle in his voice.

Someone else would have to spruce up the Venn diagram. A tectonic plate had just slammed into my future. I left work early—taking a half sick day—and holed up at the Espresso Bar on Christopher Street. I bummed a cigarette, wrote in my journal, and frothed.

Why did the judge ask him to adopt the baby? Did she see something in Danny that made her think he'd be a suitable father? Did she know he was gay and in a relationship? Why wasn't the baby already placed with a family? There had to be other families waiting—ready, willing, and able to take a baby, especially a healthy newborn. Why was the judge bypassing them? And why did Danny say yes without consulting me first? What was he thinking?

LOST

Danny and I had never discussed becoming parents. Not seriously. We knew it wasn't practical or realistic, so we didn't indulge in magical thinking. This topic had only come up once during our three years together, in passing. The conversation went something like this:

Danny: Ever thought about kids?

Me: I think about my nephews all the time.

Danny: No, I mean us having a kid.

Me: Not really. I don't see how that's possible.

Danny: Not now. In the future.

Me: Like when we're forty or something?

Danny: I don't know.

Me: It costs a lot of money. I suppose we could start saving now, so we have the option later. If by the time we turn forty, we haven't saved enough or changed our minds, we can use the money to travel or something else.

That was it. We never spoke again about starting a family nor did we start a fund for kids or travel. Without seed money, it seemed unlikely our future would include children.

When Danny came home from work, he said a quick hello to Joe and headed straight to the bedroom. He sat on the edge of the bed, looking excited like a child eager to share everything he had learned at school that day. It was clear that our minds were in different places. While I worried about the ramifications, he fantasized about the possibilities.

As soon as Danny finished telling me about his day in court, I immediately responded, "It's not a good idea. We're not ready."

He didn't expect such a response. Maybe he hoped for enthusiasm. Maybe eagerness. Perhaps confusion and concern. But he certainly didn't anticipate outright rejection. I could see his spirit visibly deflate before my eyes.

"We can make it work," he said.

"How?" I asked.

"I don't know."

"We don't live alone."

"We can change that."

"I don't want to." Once again, Danny looked crushed. In just a matter of minutes, the man he loved and wanted to spend his life with had rejected his vision of the future.

"I understand you're concerned," he said.

"Do you?" I asked.

"I do. It's a big step."

"Life-changing, Danny. I don't want my life to change. Look around. We don't have the space or resources."

"Resources?"

"Money. It takes a lot of money."

"Not really," Danny said. "The baby is actually free."

"Sure, the acquisition is free, but do you have any idea how much it costs to raise a child?"

"We can cut back on expenses. Cook more, eat out less. We can make this work." The more he insisted that we could make it work, the angrier and more confused I became, especially by his newfound assertiveness. Danny had always been the most unassuming person I knew, almost mindfully unaware at times. But now, he seemed utterly lucid and present.

"What were you thinking?" I asked. "Why in the world did you say yes?"

"What was I supposed to say?" he replied.

"How about 'Thanks for asking. Let me think about it, talk it over with my partner, and get back to you?'"

"Isn't that what I'm doing now?"

"But you already said yes."

I don't like losing arguments. Danny, on the other hand, doesn't like arguing, period. He doesn't have the drive to be right or validated like I do. He simply states his viewpoint without hyperbole, drama, or escalation. Most arguments with him are unsatisfying.

"What if I want to produce another play?" I asked.

"So then you produce another play," he said.

"I'd have to write one first. How am I going to do that with a baby around?"

"You'll figure it out," he replied calmly.

"I'll figure it out? I'm glad you have so much confidence in my ability," I responded with a tinge of sarcasm.

"You're welcome," he said with a smile meant to disarm.

"I don't want to figure it out!"

"Okay," Danny said. "Then we'll figure it out."

We can make it work. We'll figure it out. His nonchalant assuredness ticked me off.

If I had been able to step back, I would have had to admit he was right. As intelligent and capable men, we could figure out the logistics. We would adjust, learn how to raise a kid, and become good parents. My resistance wasn't a matter of ability but a lack of desire to upend our lives. In that moment, objectivity betrayed me.

The walls of the bedroom felt like they were closing in. We could have debated all night and still gotten nowhere. Past midnight, Danny got into bed, ready to sleep.

"I don't want us to go to bed upset with each other," he said.

His desire to put on a happy face made me want to erupt, but instead, I put on my sneakers and tied them tightly.

"Where are you going?" he asked.

"Out."

"Really?"

"Well, you're ready for bed, and I can't sleep. We're not going to resolve this, and so…I… it's best I go for a walk."

I grabbed my coat and left. I needed the brisk December air to cool me off.

New York is called the city that never sleeps, but on frigid weekdays after midnight, it takes a solid power nap. No one else was out, at least not on the sidewalks. The emptiness exhilarated and spooked me at the same time. Steam rose from the manholes like intoxicated ghosts trying to escape hell. With headphones on, I drowned myself in music that had always provided solace, inspiration, or distraction from my internal turmoil: Bruce Springsteen, Mary Chapin Carpenter, Indigo Girls, Stevie Nicks. I tramped down to the West Village, then east, then north to Chelsea, and back.

Scenes from childhood played out in my mind, particularly memories of family gatherings in the late 1970s in Greenpoint, where my dad grew up. I remembered the men—my father, uncles, and cousins—joking about their parental responsibilities. "You made them, you suffer," they'd say to one another with gusto and boisterous laughter. Though I knew they loved their kids and didn't mean what they said, my younger self internalized the message that children were a burden.

I walked for miles that night and analyzed how a baby would impact every second of every minute of every hour of every day. It wasn't all negative. In many ways, the timing couldn't have been better. Free from the demanding schedules of the show and campaign, Danny and I stared at a blank slate on which to write our next chapter. But I was far from ready to turn the page into parenthood. What did it really mean to be a parent? What would it be like to have a baby be a part of everything we did? Who would we become? As gay dads, what kind of obstacles would we face? Did I possess the patience, tenderness, and consistency to be an effective father? And who did we think we were to be this miracle baby's parents?

What if we messed up? One parent had already failed Baby Ace. He didn't need us to compound that original indignity. He deserved better. With our limited resources and space, I doubted we could provide a better life.

The truth is, I was scared. My biggest fear was being inadequate and unworthy of a child, especially this one. How would I handle it when this child eventually tugged at my pants with questions I couldn't answer? What if I gave the wrong answers? I was afraid of everything—being imperfect, getting too close, and the eventual heartbreak of having to one day let him go. Bottom line, I was petrified of loving so deeply and completely.

Fear and worry were ingrained in me, woven into my DNA from the moment of conception. My mother had suffered a nervous breakdown and long depression after losing a child just before me—a boy who was delivered stillborn. I was conceived during this difficult period, so my umbilical cord was nothing more than a frayed nerve. As a result, worry became a dominant character trait for me.

I arrived home late, after 2 am. The walk had done some good. Exhaustion took the edge off, and I crawled into bed to snuggle next to Danny. His warmth thawed off the night. I slept well and woke up later than usual. We carried on with our typical morning routine and didn't get a chance to discuss anything before leaving for work.

At the office, I couldn't concentrate. I stared blankly at the computer screen. The pixels huddled close, whispering and conspiring. The day dragged on.

After work, back in the four walls of our bedroom, I restarted our discussion about the baby.

"Did you tell anyone?" I asked.

"No. You?"

"No. Well, yesterday, after you called, I did share the news with a few coworkers. Maya knows."

"What does she think?" he asked.

"It doesn't matter." Of course, I couldn't reveal what she had actually said—that we have to do it. I preferred to keep the news contained. We didn't need the opinions of the entire world. This was our decision, and I believed we should make it without external influence. Honestly, I didn't want my friends or family to perceive me as an ungrateful jerk for being on the fence. Since I already saw myself that way, letting others pile on was unnecessary.

"Let's keep this to ourselves for now," I said. Danny nodded. It was the first thing related to the baby we had agreed on.

"Just so you know," he said, "I'm going to pursue adopting the baby with or without you."

"So you're choosing a baby over our relationship?"

"No," he said.

"That's exactly what you're doing."

"Pete, I'd love for you to do this with me, but I understand if you're not ready."

"Good luck being a single parent in New York City," I said. The sarcastic threat didn't faze him. Why would it? He didn't share my doubts. He was certain everything would work itself out. But the more certain he was, the more uncertain I became.

"I just think it's an opportunity we can't pass up." He made it sound like a promotion or a career move—an offer with more money and a corner office. But corner offices, like babies, came with greater responsibility. I didn't want to be responsible.

"All I've been doing is obsessing over how a baby is going to affect our lives," I said. "I'm taking this very seriously. You're not."

"I am," he said.

"Who's going to be home with him at least two days a week? Me. I will be the one tending to every single one of his needs. You know this is going to affect me way more than you."

He nodded, conceding that point, but then calmly raised the stakes.

"The foster care agency needs us to complete some paperwork and get fingerprinted. It's all standard stuff. They're arranging a visit with the baby. Gail has to get back to me with a date and time. Look, even if you don't want to adopt, I would love for you to be there with me."

I didn't answer.

"Just think about it," he said. "We'll never get a chance like this again."

The debate was over for him. We both knew it. The fight was between me and me. So, once again, for the second night in a row, I left to pound the pavement.

PROS AND CONS

The next morning, I woke up desperate for a sounding board, another voice other than my own. I had always relied on a support system that included my sister and two friends, Chuck and Dean. No matter what they had to say, it couldn't be any worse than the echo chamber of pushy know-it-alls in my head.

I called Linda first. She wasn't just my sister; she was my confidant and best friend. But it wasn't always that way, especially when we were in high school together. Linda was a popular senior, a cheerleader. As a freshman, I lived in her shadow, feeling awkward and invisible. And I resented her. When she was nominated for Homecoming Queen, I told all my friends not to vote for her. Word got out, and she ended up losing by two votes. It was definitely my fault.

My role in that election is why I worked tirelessly to get her elected to Congress in 2000. She had plenty of people trying to control her appearance, speech, and actions — self-appointed handlers—so she often turned to me to remind her of who she truly was and why she wanted to serve the public. I dropped everything to help her through campaign challenges, listen when she needed to sort through all the voices, or simply vent.

Now, I needed her to do the same for me.

"What's up, Lollie?" Linda knew it was me calling.

"Not much, Lollie," I replied.

Our conversations always started with the nickname "Lollie." We picked it up as kids from our nanny, our grandmother on Mom's side. She called everyone "Lollie." Linda and I eventually adopted it as our own term of endearment.

I went on to tell Lollie all about Danny, the judge, and the baby. She listened without interrupting until I mentioned that the judge asked Danny to adopt.

"Wait, wait, wait. Back up. The judge did what?" She interrupted.

"You heard me right. She asked him if he wanted to adopt the baby," I repeated.

"Oh my god, are you joking?"

When I didn't say anything, she sensed my fear and trepidation and toned down her excitement for my sake.

Then we got tactical, doing what we always did when faced with tough decisions: We made a list of pros and cons.

Pros	Cons
• The baby and all the joy, love, and happiness he will bring	• Losing my identity and freedom
	• Overbearing responsibility
• Experiencing the world anew through his eyes	• Giving up theater company, writing, softball, bowling, gym, movies and plays
• Grandkids, someday	• Going into debt
	• No more spontaneity, happy hours, spur-of-the-moment, last-minute anything
	• Not sleeping
	• Failing: ruining the baby's life
	• Constant worrying

While this side-by-side comparison had been helpful during the campaign, it now seemed like a trite, two-dimensional, quantitative assessment that did little to help solve a complex, three-dimensional, and existential dilemma. Despite the cons outnumbering the pros, the comparison proved useless. The columns weren't columns at all; they were more like two sides of a balance scale. No matter how many reasons I piled onto the con side, it still tipped in favor of the pro side, which held the baby. Fears are hollow. Hope is dense. I even had to admit that the downside was actually the upside.

Linda acknowledged the validity of my concerns, but then, like a good lawyer, she systematically dissected, disputed, and dismissed everything on the con side as irrational worries that could be overcome.

"Don't overthink it," she said. "Ultimately, it's a choice only you can make, but I would do it if I were you. And I have no doubt you and Danny would make great dads."

It wasn't exactly what I wanted to hear, but I appreciated the feedback. And I probably shouldn't have expected anything different. Linda adored Danny.

They met shortly after he and I began dating in the summer of 1997. The three of us were trying to get inside Central Park to see Garth Brooks, but we never got close. So, instead, we did the next best thing: We headed to Cowgirl, our favorite Tex-Mex restaurant in the West Village.

Linda and Danny hit it off instantly. They were both born in 1965, inaugural Generation Xers. But that's not what bonded them. What bonded them was Texas. Linda had lived in Dallas for six months in the early '90s, and that's all they talked about. I was relieved they got along so well so quickly. The next day, Linda called to give me the stamp of approval. "Lollie," she said, "he's a keeper."

After speaking with Linda and discarding the pros and cons list, I opened my bedroom window to let in some fresh air. The frame, warped and bent, barely kept the pane from crashing to the ground. Across the street, The Vermeer, a bulky, luxurious apartment building, mocked those of us who lived in what I had nicknamed The Vermin. Doormen greeted residents of The Vermeer. Door rats greeted us. This was no place to raise a child.

* * *

That night, as Danny and I prepared for bed, he informed me that he had asked the guy subletting his apartment to move out.

"Either we can live there, or Joe can," he said.

"Are there good schools up there?" I asked.

"I don't know," Danny said. "He's an infant."

"What about daycare?"

"I don't know," he said.

"These are things we need to know, we need to think about and plan for."

I turned out the light, stared into the darkness, and added a tick mark to my side of the debate scorecard – the one that existed only in my head.

The next day, after work, I met up with Chuck, my right-hand man at the theatre company. He directed our debut production in March and acted in the most recent one that just ended. We met for a drink every week—yet another thing I would have to give up.

"You have to do it," he said after I explained the situation. "It's not every day that a baby just falls into your lap like this."

"I know, it's just…"

"Come on. It'll be an adventure. What are you afraid of?"

"Everything."

"Let me ease your mind about one thing," he said. "If you're worrying about the theatre company, don't. We'll have plenty of opportunities to put on another show. Besides, we still need time to recover from the last one."

In his way, Chuck was telling me to get over myself. He insisted we had to adopt. And then he took it one step further.

"When you get him," he said, "I'll watch him once a week. You and Danny pick a night, and I'm there." His offer to babysit once a week caught me off guard, and my eyes welled up.

But his offer came with one condition.

"Don't even think about moving to Jersey with that kid. He's a New Yorker. For Christ's sake, Danny found him on the subway. You have to raise him here. He deserves that. I was raised in the city and turned out fine." Anticipating a sarcastic reply, he preemptively waved a finger in my face. "Don't say a word."

At that point, the tally had three votes in favor—Maya, Linda, and Chuck—and zero opposed.

All three buttressed the part of me that was genuinely enamored and curious about becoming a dad. I began to see glimpses of a fantastic future with a son and a family: visions of playing catch on grassy fields, orange-sky picnics along the waterfront, Christmas mornings, makeshift blanket forts, hide and seek, and bedtime stories. Time skipped ahead ten years, then back three, and forward again. The glimpses advanced and retreated, expanded and contracted, each a vivid vision of a future fuller than the present.

The pros were winning.

Until they weren't.

The next night, I saw my friend Dean. Fifteen years my senior, he was my gay father figure. Be it boy trouble, confusion about life, or creative struggles, a chat with Dean always cleared things up. We spent countless nights at his place drinking merlot, eating Chinese takeout, and sorting through personal and professional problems, mostly mine. Originally from Shreveport, Louisiana, his voice still carried traces of a Southern accent, and like most of my other friends, he called me Petey, although with his slight drawl, it sounded more like Pee-Dee.

I picked up a bottle of cheap red wine on my way to his place. We cracked it open, and a few sips later, I was spilling my guts.

"Don't do it, Petey. It's a big mistake if you ask me." Dean didn't mince words. "Think about the baby. That poor kid is going to have to explain to people for the rest of his life why he has two dads and no mother."

I had expected him to give me measured and constructive advice, as he had done many times before. But instead, he strongly opposed our adoption.

"It's not fair to the baby," he said. "He doesn't look like either of you. That's not going to be easy for him later in life."

Later in life? Slow down.

The fact that Baby Ace wouldn't look like Danny or me didn't even rank on my list of excuses. My two nephews were Asian and looked nothing like my brother and sister-in-law. Danny also had three adopted siblings, an adopted nephew and a niece. Baby Ace would become another member of a diverse, multiracial family with adopted relatives. If any issues about being adopted arose later in life, his older cousins would be there for him. Our extended families were well-prepared to handle any situation that might come up.

When I pushed back, Dean tried a different approach.

"Where are you going to live? You can't raise a baby in that dump. You'll be living like the Buckets in Willy Wonka."

I chuckled.

"And another thing," he continued, expanding his argument, "I don't understand this new trend, fad, whatever, of gay men wanting to have babies."

I nodded. Neither did I. On that point, we agreed.

"I hope babies don't become the new Dalmatians," I joked, trying to lighten the mood. "Remember a few years ago when every Chelsea boy had to have a Dalmatian or be seen with one? Now the dogs are gone. Where did they all go? It's a mystery."

"It's not a mystery at all," Dean replied. "I'll tell you what happened. The dogs became inconveniences. The fad ended. And now it's babies. Listen, if it were up to me, nobody would be allowed to have a baby until someone explains what happened to all those Dalmatians." We laughed and washed down the absurdity with more wine. "It's not your job to rescue this baby again," he said, adopting a more conciliatory tone. "He'll be fine with another family."

"I know," I agreed. "And I don't want to feel like we have to rescue him. I don't want that to be our motivation, you know?"

"All I know is you just started Other Side Productions. Your baby is your work. Your writing. The theatre company. Think about Chuck and Jackie and Maya and Lanie and l'il ol' me. You've already created a family. We're counting on you to keep it going. I didn't sweat for eight weeks in a cramped sound booth for nothing."

Dean fed and empowered my hungry internal naysayers. And by playing up the theatre company as my family, he jabbed at my most exposed nerve. Would Baby Ace force me to give up my dreams? Maybe I should just let Danny turn his life upside down—rearrange it any way he wished—move back to Morningside Heights, find daycare, and endure sleepless nights with a screaming baby on his own. Let him figure it out. Let him make it work. I was sure he and Baby Ace would be just fine and probably even better off without me.

I didn't want our relationship to end. But if Danny proceeded with the adoption without me, how could it survive?

I decided that a clean break would be in everyone's best interest—his, mine, and the baby's.

My heart sank.

PRINCE AND THE PEA

On my way home from Dean's, my mind was filled with memories of how Danny and I first met.

In the spring of 1997, I and about fifteen new recruits, including my soon-to-be roommate Joe, joined the Big Apple Softball League draft. Typically, new players were assigned to existing teams, but since there were enough recruits, the league officers decided to create an all-rookie team. At our first practice, we aptly named ourselves the "Rookies."

Most of our games were Sunday morning double-headers. And we lost. A lot. Blowouts. We took the losses in stride and focused on the social aspects of the league—going bar-hopping on Christopher Street after the games, with the final stop at our sponsor bar, the Dugout, a musky, no-frills dive joint on the outskirts of the West Village.

One of my teammates, Oscar, was friends with Danny in Texas. He invited Danny to all our games and other team activities. Secretly, Oscar wanted us to hook up, but I hardly noticed Danny.

Fresh out of a three-year relationship that started right after I came out and having only been involved with one guy, that spring and early summer was finally my time to sow some oats. Post-games at the Dugout were freedom to me. A place rife with sexual tension, where I flirted with other men for the first time in my life. But the embroidered "Rookies" across my jersey not only represented my team affiliation—it also described my hooking-up acumen.

On and off the field, I hit a ton of singles and only reached first base. At the Dugout, I drank beer after beer, then kissed and made out quite often. But all the kissing came with a cost. I contracted mono. At 29 years old, I caught the teenage kissing disease. As a result, my lips were benched until further notice. But despite my setback, I still loved Sundays.

Encouraged by Oscar, Danny continued to hang around the Rookies and attended our games. He scouted me throughout May and June, but I had no clue. He operated in my blind spot. His blip never made it onto my radar. Just as he was about to give up on catching my attention, Danny made one final attempt.

After a sweltering ninety-degree doubleheader in mid-July, Danny seized an opportunity when he noticed me at the Dugout's jukebox, browsing through song selections. Chumbawamba's "Tubthumping" ended, and Third Eye Blind's "Semi-Charmed Life" started playing. I searched for country music options and stumbled upon Garth Brooks' *Greatest Hits*. I put in a few dollars to queue up a block of his songs, including "Standing Outside the Fire," "The Thunder Rolls," "Friends in Low Places," "The Dance," and "Two of a Kind, Workin' on a Full House."

As I punched in the last digits, Danny approached me and asked, "Can I get you a beer?"

"Not drinking," I said, "getting over a bad cold." My first words to him, a lie.

He walked away. A minute later, he handed me a bottled water—a clutch pinch hit. His thoughtful gesture changed everything. He was no longer in my blind spot. He was right in front of me in living color.

Up close, the crevasses left by adolescent acne scars made his face look like the surface of a sponge (his description, not mine). But the scars also chiseled his face, giving him a rugged, masculine allure. Combined with his thick salt-and-pepper hair, he was strikingly good-looking. Why hadn't I noticed him sooner? While the lines across his face made him appear serious and somewhat harsh, he was anything but.

When I finished one bottle of water, he bought me another—and then another. His patience and persistence paid off. It took nearly three months, a bout with an adolescent disease, and several bottles of water for his blip to capture my attention.

Because Danny matched each of my bottled waters with a vodka and cranberry, he didn't remember much of our conversation. But I did. We laughed a lot over the fact that he, a native Texan, didn't listen to country music, but I, a native New Yorker, did. I invited him to go two-stepping and asked him if he wanted to come with me to see Garth Brooks in Central Park. We didn't kiss at the bar, but there was a spark.

Long after the sun went down, I suggested we leave the bar and go for a walk. He needed to sober up. I slung his rollerblades over one shoulder and my duffle bag over the other. We stepped out into the heat of the night and have been together ever since.

That summer, I not only gained a family of Rookies—my brothers—but also found the love of my life. And Danny, after staying silent in the shadows, found his voice—a loud one. He screamed his lungs out whenever I came to bat for the rest of the season.

"Peter! Peter! Hit the ball like Derek Jeter!"

If only.

* * *

But now, three years later, that summer was nothing but a distant memory.

The metal apartment door screeched as I pushed it open, then banged shut when I shoved it to close. The front door abutted the partition that divided the living room, behind which Joe slept on a loft platform. While the partition looked like a real wall, it stopped two feet short of the ceiling. The noise and bleeding light from the hallway must have woken him up. A true friend, Joe never complained when I came in late.

I tiptoed in the dark to the bedroom. Danny had one eye open, and one eye closed. I sat on the edge of the bed and looked wistfully at the exposed top half of his curled-up body.

This is it. This is how it ends.

I wanted to hash things out right then and there and come to some sort of resolution, but I was tapped out. All I could say was, "We need to talk."

"It's late," he said. "Get in bed. We'll talk tomorrow?" He folded over the blanket on my side, his outstretched arm an invitation to spoon.

"Tomorrow's fine," I said, grateful for the reprieve as I rested my head on his chest, under his chin. Stubble pricked my forehead. Before drifting off, a knot pinged in my stomach. Would it be the last time we snuggled? In less than twenty-four hours, everything could change in our relationship. We might end up as just friends or casual acquaintances. Since I didn't want to become a parent, I couldn't see how we'd be able to stay together as a couple. I cherished the night like it might be our last together.

The next morning, a Saturday, my dad called. Still half asleep and groggy, I flopped my arm over to pick up the phone.

"Hello?"

"Peter?" he shouted.

"Yeah."

"It's your father."

Like clockwork, Dad called every Thursday (sometimes Friday) night to find out if our weekend plans included visiting them in New Jersey. Most weekends, it did, but he liked to confirm our plans days in advance. This was a rare Saturday morning call.

"My father who?" I joked.

"Yeah, yeah," he chuckled. "Look, are you gonna be around later? Your mother and I are coming in to see a matinee and… What are you guys doing for dinner?"

"No plans," I said, although I didn't know what our relationship status would be by then.

"Is everything all right?" he asked.

"Yeah, why?"

"Oh, because I called last night, and no one answered."

"Did you leave a message?"

"I don't leave messages." It had been almost two decades since the dawn of the answering machine, but my parents were still uncomfortable with the technology.

"Listen," Dad continued, "I'm going to park by you so I can come up to use the bathroom before the show."

With my parents on the way, the heart-to-heart conversation I wanted to have with Danny would have to wait.

As usual, Joe was up early and already out of the apartment. But he left us a present. The scent of freshly brewed coffee filled the apartment, and he had left a pot on the burner for us. I went to the kitchen, poured two mugs, tucked the early parts of Joe's Sunday *New York Times* under my arm, and returned to the bedroom. I turned on the 5-CD disc changer and set it to shuffle songs in the background. Danny sat up and smiled at me for bringing him coffee in bed. He inhaled the aroma, blew on the brim of the mug, and took a sip. I separated the newspaper sections, gave him the Real Estate and Styles sections, and kept the Sports and Arts for myself. There we were, looking like a living advertisement for the *Times*. It was an image of domestic bliss that begged for a child bouncing on the bed to complete the scene.

I couldn't bring myself to talk about the baby or our relationship. Besides, the urgency had worn off after a good night's sleep. I scanned the hockey scores. The Devils beat the Canadiens.

My parents' visit raised my antenna. Was something else going on? Were they really going to see a play? Or did my sister spill the beans about the baby? One look at their cat-ate-the-canary faces, and I'd have an answer.

Danny showered and dressed before me. Just as I exited the bathroom, our intercom buzzed. My parents had arrived even earlier than my dad had mentioned.

I didn't get a good read on my dad before he disappeared into the bathroom. Wherever he went, using the restroom was always his first order of business. Mom seemed like she might be withholding something, but I couldn't be sure. She dropped her tote onto the table and greeted Danny and me with kisses on the cheek. Within moments of arriving anywhere, my parents had a knack for taking over the space and spreading out.

"Did you guys eat?" Mom asked as she dug up two foil-wrapped sandwiches from her bag. The great thing about my parents was that you never had to feed them; they always brought food wherever they went. This particular day's lunch consisted of turkey breast on a seedless roll with lettuce and mayo. "You want half?"

"No, we're good," I said.

"We got lucky," Dad emerged from the bathroom. "Clear sailing all the way through the tunnel. And then a guy pulled out of a spot on 15th Street." Dad unwrapped his sandwich. "Louise, did you put mustard on mine?"

"This one's yours, Sam." The mundane chatter about traffic, parking, and mustard convinced me they were clueless about the baby. Since we had just finished eating, we sat and watched my parents eat.

Mom proceeded to update us on the latest "sick and dying" report, her detailed account of who had contracted what illness, often cancer, and who had succumbed to what disease, cancer again. Even though I didn't personally know most of the people mentioned in her report, she still felt compelled to tell me. She seemed to relish in spreading sad news. The more tragic the story, the better. If a narrative lacked tragedy, she would find a way to embellish it until it reached catastrophic proportions. And her compulsion to recite the report took precedence over whatever you might be doing at the time. I can't recall the specifics of that day's report, but a typical one would build up suspense and go something like this:

"You remember Pauline Freeman?" she would ask.

"Who?"

"Mrs. Freeman? Your crossing guard from elementary school."

"Mom," I'd say, "can't you see I'm in the middle of reading a book?"

"Oh," she'd snipe, offended. "Well, she died."

Mom had a habit of exaggerating illnesses. You couldn't even sniffle around her without being diagnosed with sinus cancer or anemia, another of her favorite go-to diseases. When I was seventeen and discovered a hard, pea-sized lump on my left testicle, Mom immediately had me dying of cancer. Funeral arrangements played out in her head—what I would wear in the casket, which passages my siblings would read during the church service, and even who would be responsible for designing the photo collage.

Embarrassed by the pea's location, I implored Mom to keep it private. But that was asking too much. The next day, my Aunt Rosie called. As my dad's only sibling and my only aunt, she had a habit of dropping f-bombs into any conversation. But the way she spoke to me, using somber, hushed tones as if trying not to wake the nearly-dead, made it clear that Mom had blabbed. While news delivered via the "Lou-phatic" system always metastasized, luckily, the pea never did.

Dad changed the subject, a gnashed-up turkey sandwich partially stuffed in his cheeks like a chipmunk, mumbling, "We met a couple this week at PFLAG who are taking in three biological siblings..."

"So they don't get separated," Mom finished his sentence. "And they already have five foster kids. I don't know how they do it. The new ones are Mexican."

"Louise," Dad interrupted, "they had only two before, and their new..."

"So that makes five," she cut in.

"Their new kids aren't Mexican. They're from Guatemala."

"Okay, whatever it is."

These kinds of interactions happened all the time. One would initiate a conversation with you; then the other would chime in, turning it into a private discussion between themselves, with you as a spectator.

While I grew up accustomed to Mom's tendencies to embellish and their habit of sharing everything out loud, Danny was not. He felt obligated to show interest, and that's why Mom liked him. A lot. And honed in on him, wanting a reaction to whatever tale she peddled. He was her prince, the golden boy who could do no wrong. In Mom's eyes, I never treated him like royalty. Whenever she heard me playfully tease him about being a Southerner, she'd get protective, saying, "Leave my Danny alone!"

He was more hers than mine. He was good. I was bad. But I held information that she didn't. Something that could shatter her blind protection of my boyfriend. He had once made lasagna with cottage cheese. I kept that unforgivable sin in my back pocket, just in case I ever needed to use it to help her get over our breakup.

Before Mom and Dad left for the matinee, they asked Danny where he would like to have dinner for his birthday the next day. I nearly gasped. I had been so self-absorbed all week that I had forgotten his birthday. Danny deftly deferred to my dad. By then, he had learned we would end up eating where Dad wanted anyway.

I followed my parents out and snuck off to The Gap and a card shop in the village. A flannel shirt, boxers, a funny card, a heartfelt card, and dinner with my folks would have to suffice. After buying the gifts, I grabbed a coffee from the Espresso Bar and walked to the waterfront.

Like a smooth sheet of reflective glass extending all the way to Hoboken, the Hudson River was still and tranquil. And that's when my better angels spoke up: *Do you know how many people would kill to trade places with you? Danny is right. The two of you will never get a chance like this again. This baby is a gift. He's the best thing that's happened in your life. You don't know it yet. But trust us, you will.*

After dinner and hearing all about the play and the theatre's uncomfortable seats, we showed my parents to their car. After a hug and kiss goodbye, Danny and I headed back home.

"You know what," I said. "Let's walk around a bit."

"Sure," Danny replied.

We turned back the other way on Fifteenth Street. Our usual stroll—what we called the Chelsea loop—took us across Fifteenth Street, up Eighth Avenue to 23rd Street, then back down Seventh Avenue to The Vermin. Somewhere around Baby Ace's corner, I decided to bring up the topic that had been left unaddressed.

"We need to talk about what we're not talking about," I said.

"I was giving you space," he said.

"I know, I know," I said with a gentler tone. "I appreciate that. I really do. And despite all my flipping out, I want you to know I'm not completely against doing this."

"I know you're not," he said.

"It irked the hell out of me that adopting the baby seemed like a done deal for you regardless of how I felt."

"I'm sorry," he said, "that wasn't my intention. I know this is a big life decision."

"The biggest," I said. "How were you able to make it so fast?"

We paused in front of Roger & Dave, a quirky card and gift shop on Eighth Avenue near 21st Street. Danny's friend who worked there waved at us through the window. Danny waved back and then answered my question.

"I guess when the judge asked," he said, "I saw it as a gift. And so I just said 'yes.' I didn't consider the difficulties or challenges. It just felt right—the right thing to do. I don't know, Pete. I also think the seed to become a parent was planted right after finding the baby. People kept asking me, 'Why didn't you just take him home?' As if the baby was a lost puppy. But then others asked point blank, 'Why don't you adopt him?' I knew that was impossible. The steps and legal procedures would… It wasn't viable. But the thought of 'why not?' nagged at me. I knew in my heart I wanted to be a parent someday. So here was an opportunity, a gift. And then I saw a future with us as a family, rich with love. From the mundane to the divine and everything in between, just completeness."

As I listened, my defenses began to melt away. Danny had embraced the baby as a gift of fate, and in that moment, so did I. He was right. Saying yes was the right thing to do. Danny wasn't dismissing me. He was welcoming our destiny with open arms. I got chills and felt a surge of emotion. Something greater than us was in control, guiding our path. All I had to do was surrender.

We kept walking.

"Just so you know," Danny said, "I'm scared too."

"Now you tell me."

"I don't know what the future holds, Pete, but I'm confident we'll handle whatever comes our way. One day at a time."

It's something I wished he had expressed the first time we talked. Maybe he did, and I didn't hear him, or maybe I didn't want to hear him.

"The visit is scheduled for Thursday," he said. "Come with me."

"I don't know," I said.

"You don't have to commit to anything. It's not like they can give him to us right away. It's going to take months, maybe even a year. So we'll have plenty of time to adjust and prepare."

I nodded.

Danny took my hand. We turned the corner onto Seventh Avenue, the final stretch.

We were now heading in the same direction.

Home.

Together.

A VIEW OF THE BRIDGE

Thursday, December 14, 2000

My stomach churned the second I woke up on the day we were supposed to visit Baby Ace. I went to work but told my supervisor I needed to leave early. Danny also left work early, and we met at Talbot Perkins around 3:45 pm.

Baby Ace had been placed with a family living in one of the so-called Bridge apartments that straddle the roadway at the end of the George Washington Bridge. Gail couldn't make it, so Cheryl, a younger and less experienced caseworker from the agency, accompanied us during the visit. She was mellower than mellow and moved like a sloth without a care in the world. Danny said her demeanor was the opposite of Gail's, who he had described as engaging, vibrant, and full of life. Cheryl seemed as though she had just woken up. But since it was late, we assumed her tiredness was due to a long and demanding work day.

"I don't know why ACS thinks this is an unfit home," Cheryl commented as we entered the vestibule. She pressed the buzzer.

No one answered. She pressed again. After her third attempt, we entered as someone exited. Although Danny had previously visited clients living in public housing complexes, this was my first time inside. At first glance, it didn't seem much different from where we lived. The dirt-smudged walls and dim lighting matched the decor in The Vermin. So in a way, it reminded me of home, but not really. I viewed our living situation as temporary and hoped to move somewhere nicer eventually. The residents coming and going from the Bridge apartments didn't seem to share the same sense of hope. This may have been their "somewhere nicer."

We waited five minutes for the only working elevator to reach the ground floor. Once inside, it crawled upward, scraping against the shaft with a sound of metal on metal. I clutched the railing as if it could protect me in case of a sudden drop. When we finally reached our floor, the elevator doors opened to reveal a long, dingy hallway that reeked of deep fryer grease. Cheryl paused and knocked on a door midway down the hall. We could hear children's voices, the pitter-patter of little feet, and movements inside, but nobody answered.

"MS. GARCIA!" Cheryl shouted and knocked again. The door finally opened. A hairy man wearing sagging boxers and no shirt stood in the doorway, looking annoyed. A young girl clung to one of his bushy thighs, making it hard to tell where her head ended and his leg began. She kept one eye behind the bottom of his underwear and the other on us.

"His wife didn't tell him about our visit," Cheryl explained. "She's at the doctor's with the other kids and will be back soon. But we're going to wait. Let's go inside."

The man, whom I assumed was Mr. Garcia, moved aside to let us in. He closed the door behind us, mumbled a few words in Spanish under his breath, and then disappeared into the bedroom. Other children peeked in, their heads slanted from behind the corner.

Cheryl gestured to the living room, and we moved further into the apartment.

A dozen or more stories up, we had a bird's-eye view west. The lights of the George Washington Bridge's east column and arching cables reflected in the Hudson River, glistening in the dark yet peaceful river. Inside stood an artificial Christmas tree with colored lights flashing in sparse chunks. One section didn't flash at all, and the perfectionist in me tensed up. How could you not fix that? I wanted to yank all the lights off, test every bulb, fix the duds, and then restring them uniformly.

The chaos continued above the tree. Drop-ceiling panels were missing or askew as if an earthquake had shaken them off the brackets. Underneath, two extension cords snaked around and through dust mounds. One cord powered the lights. The other plugged into an outlet but remained unconnected on the open end. I had a sudden panicked image of Baby Ace's electrocution or strangulation. Now, not only did I want to fix the lights and straighten the ceiling, but I also wanted to dust, vacuum, disinfect, unplug the extra cord, and baby-proof the entire apartment.

"Have a seat, guys," Cheryl said.

Danny sat on the sofa, crossed his legs, and made himself comfortable. He looked like he could have been waiting for the bus, waiting at the dentist's office, waiting for Guffman, or even worse, waiting for Godot. If he was tense in any way, it didn't show. It never does. Once again, his calm demeanor made my anxiety seem disproportionately exaggerated. I sat and leaned into him, hoping some of his Zen might rub off on me.

"If Cheryl thinks this is a good home, I wouldn't want to see the bad ones," I whispered in his ear.

"I know," he said.

"I wonder what her home is like."

"What do you mean?"

"Think about it. This place might be better than where she lives now." I got up. "I'm going to ask her."

"Don't!" Danny grabbed my arm.

"I want to know why she thinks this is a good home."

"Pete, please," he said, as if asking Cheryl about the current state of foster homes would ruin our chances of running one.

I glanced at my watch. 4:45. Daylight slowly descended behind the Palisades on the Jersey side of the Hudson. I worried about the foster mom being outside in the cold with Baby Ace.

A key slid into the lock, and the apartment door opened. *Here we go. We're going to meet the baby we might call "son."*

Ms. Garcia pushed in a stroller while another child held the door. Baby Ace was covered with blankets. We all stood at attention as if a dignitary had just entered. When Ms. Garcia saw Cheryl, she looked surprised. When she spotted Danny and me, her expression switched to consternation. She had forgotten about the home visit and wasn't expecting to see two white men in her living room. We were even, considering we hadn't expected to see a furry man in his undies earlier.

Cheryl and Ms. Garcia spoke in Spanish. Although Danny and I didn't understand the words, we could interpret their body language: we had just ruined her Feliz Navidad. I asked Cheryl if everything was alright, and she turned around slowly, stifling a yawn.

"Oh, don't worry. She wants to know who you guys are," Cheryl said. "Everything is fine. She's afraid you're going to take the baby. It's all fine. I told her you're not here to take the baby..." Cheryl covered her mouth so only we could see and quietly added, "Today."

Ms. Garcia took the blankets off Baby Ace, revealing the top of his brown, wispy-haired head. She released a few latches on the stroller, flipped over a handle, and lifted the seat with Baby Ace still in it. She placed it on the floor—a nifty all-in-one stroller, baby carrier, and car seat. We realized, however, that with Baby

Ace on the floor, Ms. Garcia had not physically touched him to change his location. This contact-free interaction was an unintended flaw in the seat's otherwise convenient design. Ms. Garcia parked Baby Ace in what seemed to be his designated spot on the floor, and then took off her coat.

"Could you watch him while I go over a few things with Ms. Garcia?" Cheryl asked as she slid the baby carrier closer to us.

"Sure," we both replied.

Cheryl guided Ms. Garcia back to the dining table, gestured for her to sit, and opened a folder. As they reviewed paperwork, Danny and I sat on the edge of the sofa and stared at Baby Ace. Eyes wide open without blinking, he stared right back at us. He didn't flinch or shift his determined focus. Either he was soaking us in or pleading for us to take him away in the only way he knew how.

"Hi there," Danny smiled, "remember me? I'm Danny. This is Pete." Baby Ace coughed, wet, and congested—a thickness an infant shouldn't have to break through to breathe. Cheryl turned around when she heard it.

"Would you like to hold him?" she asked.

Earlier in the day, before meeting with Cheryl, I told Danny that I didn't want to touch Baby Ace. No caressing. And definitely no holding. I was afraid of getting attached. What if the judge had second thoughts? What if they found a biological mother? I had an endless supply of unanswerable what-if questions.

"Sure, I'd love to hold him," Danny replied.

Cheryl stepped away from the table and leaned over the carrier to loosen a strap before placing the baby in Danny's arms. Danny cradled Baby Ace with both arms, flashing the biggest and widest smile I had ever seen from him. A lump caught in my throat. There was Danny, holding the baby he had found and saved, and it was the most beautiful, graceful, and miraculous thing I had ever witnessed.

They looked so natural together.

Baby Ace stared at Danny's face, studying it as if to say, "I recognize you from somewhere." Danny was clearly smitten and even more confident that adopting him was the right decision. We were going to be his parents.

"He hasn't blinked once," I said.

"Relax, he's fine," Danny responded. "He's absorbing, taking us in." Danny gestured to his messenger bag. "The camera's in my bag. Take a picture."

I fumbled to retrieve our Polaroid camera.

Danny propped up Baby Ace, faced the camera, and beamed. Baby Ace shifted his unblinking gaze in my direction. Both of their eyes were wide open, Danny's from excitement, the baby's from fear. I pressed the button, and the flash lit up the room. The sudden burst of light surprised Baby Ace, Ms. Garcia, and Cheryl.

"What was that?" Danny asked, pretending to be surprised for Baby Ace's benefit. "Did Papa just take a picture?"

"Don't call me that," I said. "It's not a done deal yet." Danny didn't react. Either he didn't hear me, or he didn't care. I shook the photo to settle my nerves.

"Your turn." He held the baby out to me. Reflexively, I extended my arms and took the bait in Danny's hands. The transfer happened quickly.

Baby Ace was heavier than I thought he would be. G-forces. His gravity pulled me in. Closer. Electromagnetism. My arms trembled. *Whatever you do, don't drop him.* And yet, while he felt heavy, I felt light. Lighter. His weight lifted the burdensome worry from my shoulders. I was rapt by the boy wrapped in my arms. I don't know how he did it, but that little devil in a onesie cast a spell on me.

"You look good, Papa," Danny said.

"Again with the 'Papa'?"

"Smile!" He took our picture and placed the developing image next to the other.

As much as my practical and reasonable brain tried to resist forming a bond, my heart was winning the battle. In my arms, Baby Ace disarmed me. He squeezed my finger, and with his longing eyes fixed on my face, a penetrating stare, and all the innocence, promise, and hope he represented, a blissful wave washed over me, engulfing my whole being with peace and warmth, filling every capillary. I felt a strange high, a contact high of floating, like an out-of-body experience. The overwhelming love instantly altered my chemistry.

Baby Ace held my finger and didn't let go. Like a reflexologist, he squeezed my pressure point, reaching the depths of my being. His grip pried open my chest, exposing my heart to my brain. Love confronted fear head-on. Baby Ace had broken through my defenses, leaving behind an open wound that surprisingly didn't hurt. No suture, staple, or bandage could be strong enough to cover or seal the hole. Besides, it wasn't something that required closure to heal.

In that moment, my natural skepticism succumbed to faith. Enough for me to believe everything was happening for a reason and that fate, after all, was in control. Danny was meant to find this baby boy. We were destined to be a family. I got it. I finally understood why Danny had said yes to the judge without hesitation. What was happening to me had happened to him in August. He had fallen in love and inextricably bonded with the baby during those sacred, uninterrupted minutes they shared alone. Before the police arrived, before the news crews arrived, before I arrived. Now it was my turn. But this time, Danny and I were together, and our precious little boy was safely cradled in my arms.

How could I have been so wrong? There was nothing to worry about. I felt brave and unafraid of what I might lose and was excited about what we were about to embrace. The future—our lives as a family, Papa, Daddy, and son—would, indeed, work itself out. And in mysterious and glorious ways.

We looked at the photos coming into focus.

Danny's expression was one I would become very familiar with in the years to come. It's the same one he's worn when the boy he's cradling in the photo would fall asleep on either of our shoulders, or call us "Dada" or "Papa" for the first time, or hold both our hands while walking down the street, or finger-paint a portrait of our family, or sing himself to sleep in the back seat of the car or learn how to ride a bike, throw a ball, play the violin, dance on stage, or more recently, tease me about going bald. Although I often wished Danny would express his emotions more openly and freely, making it easier for me to know how he's feeling, all he ever needs to do is flash that warm, contented, happy, wondrous, and loving smile that appeared many stories above the George Washington Bridge with our future son in his arms.

Life hinges on little moments, chance encounters, and happy accidents. Sometimes you find your forever, or your forever finds you, in the unlikeliest places. And although we didn't want our visit with Baby Ace to end, we couldn't wait to leave that apartment.

If only we could have taken him with us.

Soon enough.

68 THERE

FATE

Accept the things to which fate binds you, and love the people with whom fate brings you together, but do so with all your heart.

Marcus Aurelius

NEW HOPE

"We're just going to be his foster parents," Danny said on our way home. "Think of it as a trial run. If it's not for you, then it's not for you." He compared becoming a parent to test-driving a new car. But he didn't have to sell me. Still euphoric and soaring from our visit with Baby Ace, I pictured myself behind the wheel of parenthood with my foot on the accelerator.

Nevertheless, Danny was wise in pointing out the exit before we hit the highway, giving me an out I no longer wanted. The truth was, I never felt more alive or free.

As for Baby Ace, there would be no turning back once we got him. I knew we'd devote all our energy to ensuring he had a good life. Danny and I would be engaged, involved, attentive, affectionate dads, and hopefully excellent role models. This much we knew: children learn by observing their parents. So for me, that meant changing my tendency to worry. I would become confident or act as if I were. I had to seize the day now so our son could seize the day later.

As much as two men can have an unplanned pregnancy, Baby Ace was ours. He would also bind Danny and me together forever. Essentially, through our son, we'd be united like a married couple. And marriage, even a de facto one, was a sensitive subject for us.

A couple of years back, in January 1998, six months into our fledgling relationship, Danny learned about my stance on marriage the hard way. While on a snowy and icy weekend getaway at a bed & breakfast in New Hope, Pennsylvania, he got down on one knee in front of the fireplace in our room—no easy feat since he had torn his ACL a few weeks earlier.

"Pete," he said, "I know we've only been together for a short time, but I already know that I want to spend the rest of my life with you. Will you marry me?"

"The answer is no," I said. "Please get up and never ask that question again."

Regardless of one's sexual orientation, getting married is a personal choice, and personally, at the time, it wasn't for me. There was something too traditional and sanctimonious about wedlock. "Lock" being the key syllable. Yes, I loved him. But committing to spend the rest of my life with him after only six months seemed insane. Plus, in 1998, same-sex marriage was purely symbolic and not legally recognized.

Danny didn't sulk or pout. Visibly undaunted, he suggested we forget about it so we could enjoy the rest of our weekend. "I promise I'll never ask again," he said, letting the incident slide off his back. It might have been that night when Danny also learned that he just needed to be patient and wait me out when it came to important decisions.

We both thought that my rejection might end our relationship. But it didn't. Just because I didn't want to get married didn't mean I didn't want to be with him. I said "I do" and proved my love and commitment to him in other ways almost immediately.

A few days after returning from New Hope, Danny had knee surgery to repair his torn ligament. We went to the hospital at 5 am. I waited all morning for him to come out of the operating room and never left his side, even when he got sick from the morphine and threw up on me. In the following days and weeks, I used up sick and personal days at work to see him through recovery. I slept at his apartment every night until he could get up and move around without falling. Danny was neither graceful nor nimble on crutches. Outside, I braced him on the ice-covered sidewalks and became a human shield protecting him from others getting too close.

Danny and I didn't speak more about our visit with Baby Ace on the ride home from the Garcias. But our hearts ached at the thought of that bright-eyed little boy being in a neglectful home. Every bone in our bodies told us he couldn't stay there much longer without suffering psychological damage in some way. We had to do what we said we shouldn't do: rescue him.

We got off the train at Baby Ace's station and followed the same path Danny took, the one we had each taken ever since that night. We pushed through the turnstile and, without stopping, glanced at the spot where it all began. Once on the street, Danny asked, "So?"

I took a long, deep breath. "Have you thought about a name?" I asked.

Danny stopped and cracked a smile. Asking about a name meant that I had come around, moved from caution to commitment, and was invested in our future as a family.

Our new hope's name was Daniel Ace Doe, but that was also about to change.

We discussed possible names when we got home.

A last name came quickly: a hyphenated combination of ours. For a first name, neither of us wanted to keep Daniel. A child sharing a name with a parent might work for royals or George Foreman, but it didn't work for us. Besides, Daniel was my nephew's name. Having two cousins named Daniel? Three Daniels in the same family? Nope.

"How about keeping Ace?" Danny asked.

"Sounds too slick," I said. Danny agreed. Ace was out. If others nicknamed him Ace, so be it, but we wouldn't force our son to wear the moniker.

"I've always thought if I had a boy," Danny said, "I'd name him Devin."

"Oh my god," I said, "we're one letter off." He didn't know I had already given a name some thought. "Would it be okay to change the first letter to a 'K'?"

I wasn't going to quibble over one letter, but after I explained the name's significance and importance to my family and me, I was certain Danny would give up the 'D.' After all, he had left Dallas, albeit a different kind of Big D, once before; how hard could it be to leave this Big D and go with Kevin instead of Devin?

Not hard at all. He said 'Sure' without question. Daniel Ace Doe would become Kevin Stewart-Mercurio.

Later that night, before turning off the lights to sleep, I held Danny close and jokingly referred to our de facto marriage. "Don't think I'm not aware of your master plan, Mr. Stewart," I teased. "It's quite clever. Just because I said no to getting married a couple of years ago, you just went and got yourself pregnant, didn't you? Well played."

"Yeah," he said, chuckling, "if only I had thought of it sooner."

GUARDIAN ANGEL

The day after our visit, we scheduled time with Gail to complete the necessary paperwork, provide fingerprints, and begin the home study. We had no idea what to expect from the process. Danny reminded me there was no point in worrying, planning, or speculating. Gail would walk us through the steps; there was little we could do before meeting with her. Except for one thing: break the news to our families and friends.

After work, I called my parents. Since I had beaten them to their weekly Thursday night call and reversed roles by asking them about their weekend plans instead of them asking us, they assumed something was wrong.

"Is everything all right?" Dad asked.

"Everything's fine," I said. "Could you guys meet us for dinner on Saturday?"

"No problem," Dad said. "How's pizza? Your mother and I went to this place upstate last week and loved it. I mean, you don't have to get pizza. They have other things. You can get chicken parm, eggplant, pasta…"

"Sounds good," I cut him off before he recited the entire menu. "Don't invite Linda or Matthew." My sister and brother lived one town over and usually joined us for meals, but Danny and I wanted a small audience. Besides, Linda already knew about the baby.

"Why?" Dad asked. "What's wrong?"

"Nothing's wrong," I assured him. "We have news to share, and I'd rather it be just you and Mom, that's all."

"Oh, okay." He sounded confused, and when he's confused, he says, "I'll put your mother on the phone." And so he did. Now I had to repeat everything all over again. For Mom, that also meant convincing her that nobody was dying.

We didn't know exactly how my parents would react. Mom would probably be excited. Dad was the wild card. He could go either way: happy face or stern expression.

That Saturday night, the four of us squeezed into a booth at a pizzeria just north of the New Jersey–New York state line. After we ordered, Mom, who had restrained herself on the ride up, finally said, "So what's the big news?"

"Remember the baby Danny found?" I said.

"Of course," Dad said. "We keep telling that story over and over again."

"Well, we…" I stopped and turned to Danny. "I'll let you tell them."

Danny paused for a moment, then grinned and said, "We're going to become his parents."

My parents tilted their heads and sat up straighter. They couldn't tell if he was joking.

"It's true," I said. "We're going to be dads."

"Whaaaaat?" Mom asked, her voice pitched toward a shriek.

"Wait, wait, wait," Dad said, "back up a minute and start from the beginning."

Danny recounted his court appearance. At every twist in the story, Mom's jaw slackened while Dad's jaw clenched.

"Can she do that?" Mom asked after Danny finished. "I mean, legally?"

"We don't know," I said.

"You guys don't even live together."

"She knows the law better than us, Mom."

I placed the two Polaroids we had taken at the Garcias' on the table. Mom grabbed them.

"Ooooh, look at him. So precious," she said. "I can't believe it. I'm so happy." Her enthusiasm contrasted with the disbelief and concern coming from my dad.

"You know this is for the rest of your life, right?" he said.

"We know," I said.

"This is a humongous responsibility." He emphasized that and made more points about the responsibility, all of which I had already made to myself and Danny.

"Dad, we've thought this through. It's all I've been doing. Do I still have some reservations? Yes. But it's what we've decided to do."

"Twenty-four hours a day for the rest of your life," he hammered the point.

"Oh Sam, shad up already," Mom said, glowing from the pictures.

"Are you prepared?" he asked.

"Were you?" I replied.

"Let's be realistic, Peter. It takes a lot of money to raise a baby. You have money for this?"

"Did we?" Mom asked pointedly.

Dad shook his head. He was aware of the challenges that awaited.

I recalled our family visits to Greenpoint during childhood and all the times he joked, "You made them, you suffer," with his cousins. But at sixty, he was far from the young father of four who had said those words decades earlier. Sitting across from us were a man and a woman who had made many sacrifices for the sake of their children. Loving parents and upstanding citizens who volunteered, got involved in their community, and generously helped those less fortunate. They provided a safe, secure, and stable home—the building blocks and foundation from which I could go out into the world, give back, pay it forward, and create a fulfilling life. These are the unheralded, invisible gifts parents give their kids, and most kids, including myself, take them for granted. Danny and I could only hope to provide our future son with the same foundation.

"We've picked out a name," I said as a lump caught in my throat.

"Tell us! Tell us!" Mom bounced in her seat like a giddy child.

The name might cause them to relive the most painful event in their lives. Kevin was the name they had planned on giving the son they lost in 1967. And now we were naming our baby in his and their honor.

I swallowed hard to choke back my emotions.

"What's with the suspense?" Mom asked.

"It's Kevin."

Mom gasped then quickly covered her mouth to keep years of contained emotions from escaping. But she couldn't stop the tears that filled her eyes, streamed down her cheeks, and dropped to the table. Every splat carried the weight of thirty-three birthdays not celebrated. All the suppressed sadness and heartache from losing their baby came pouring out. Dad put his arm around her shoulder. Mom wiped her cheeks. The old tears of grief now mixed with new tears of joy. Kevin was coming back home.

They were speechless.

Our pizza arrived, and there was a moment of silence as the news hung in the air, mixing with the steam rising off the pies. Nobody spoke. Then, finally, Dad picked up the spatula, divvied the slices, and placed one on each of our plates.

Never in my parents' wildest imaginations could they have predicted this twist of fate. A loss like theirs, even if seldom acknowledged or talked about, remains with you for the rest of your life. And that's the funny thing about "the rest of your life": you never know its length or direction, what it might take from you, and what it might give back. And they had waited a long time for it to give something back.

Dad's colors changed like a chameleon, and his whole attitude shifted. His cautionary tale about the responsibilities of parenthood came to an end. Baby Ace now had a name—Kevin—and he approved. By the time he dove into a second slice, his jaw and shoulders had relaxed, too.

"There's something special about this kid," he said with a mouthful. "I can't quite put my finger on it, but there's something special about him."

Dad was right. Kevin was special. A mystery. The essence of an angel coming back to life.

Though I consider myself a logical and rational person, someone who requires evidence of otherworldliness, I must admit that I believe in guardian angels and that the child my parents lost before me is mine. At various low points in my life, when I desperately needed help and guidance, he revealed himself to me through other people. Some of those people were strangers, and all of them happened to be named Kevin. Mere coincidence? Perhaps. But each of those Kevins appeared in the right place at the right time, if only briefly, to save, protect, or guide me.

The little boy in the Polaroids was my reason to defy logic, relinquish reason, and let go of the need for everything to make sense. Because in this wonderfully unpredictable human experience, sometimes everything happens for a reason, and sometimes everything happens in spite of reason. Just ask my parents what they believe about Kevin's return to their lives.

Before we left the restaurant, Dad reassured us that we had their emotional and financial support.

"Don't worry about a thing," he said. "If you need anything, and I mean anything, come to us."

"Can we tell people?" Mom asked, clutching the photos tightly.

"Of course," I said as if she could keep it to herself anyway. For a change, good news would metastasize.

The next day, Danny called his mom. Conversations with her were often uncomfortable for him. His mom is a strong and opinionated woman. And while she adheres to a belief, in accordance with Southern Baptist doctrine, that the husband is the head of the household, those who know her will tell you that she is the one who truly runs the house.

He was nervous yet excited to share the news despite knowing that her fundamentalist beliefs would hinder her support. Danny's education, training in marriage and family therapy, experiences growing up gay in Texas, and faith in our ability to be great parents had all prepared him for this conversation. While he expected her response to lack full support and congratulations, he still hoped for some excitement about the good news of becoming a parent. However, Danny was also a realist and knew what her reaction would likely be.

"Danny, I think it's wonderful that you found this baby," his mom said, "but I believe a child needs both a mother and a father." Though shaken, Danny felt more resolute and confident than ever, knowing he was right and she was wrong.

"No, Mom," he said, "children need parents who will nurture and love them. That's what matters most."

Their conversations were rarely contentious, and they agreed to disagree, as they did with most issues. For a long time, Danny and his mom have maintained a respectful ongoing dialogue about his sexual orientation and her religious beliefs, even before Kevin or I entered his life.

She ended the call with "I love you."

"I love you too," Danny responded. No matter how uncomfortable some of their conversations got, they always made sure to say that, and they both genuinely meant it.

"We'll prove her wrong," Danny said after hanging up the phone. "Not out of spite or arrogance. I just know I'm right. A child needs loving, stable, attentive, affectionate, and nurturing parents, regardless of sex or gender. We're going to be great parents."

I hugged him.

At my friend Nicholas's annual tree-trimming party the next night, we gradually shared the news with a few close friends in private conversations. Some were initially skeptical, but others called it a Christmas miracle. The back slaps, high-fives, and toasts commenced. Our list of potential babysitters grew tenfold. It's too bad we didn't bring "It's a Boy" cigars to hand out or hang on the tree.

The following night, on Monday, I told my roommate Joe about our decision to adopt. I knew it would disrupt his life, so I prepared for his reaction.

"Hey, Joey, can I talk to you for a minute?" I poked my head around the partition. He was laying out clothes and packing for a morning flight to California to spend the holidays with his family.

"Sure, what's up, Petey?"

"I, um…" My hesitation caught his attention. He rolled up a T-shirt and tucked it in his suitcase. "Remember the baby Danny found…" Now Joe paused, intrigued by what I was about to say. "Well, we're going to adopt him."

"What? You're kidding, right?"

"No."

Joe slipped past me into the living room, settled onto the futon, and patted the cushion for me to join him. For the next few minutes, maybe longer, I told him everything. His eyes widened with enthusiasm. At forty-one years old, Joe still viewed the world through the eyes of a child, brimming with limitless wonder and potential. To him, this was just another testament to life's enchanting surprises.

"This is amazing!" Joe exclaimed. "I'm happy for you guys." He scooted over, wrapped his arms around me, and shook my shoulders to convey his excitement. Now, I had to break the news that we were kicking him out.

"We've decided to live here," I said.

"Oh," he said. "No problem. Petey, I totally get it."

"I'm sorry to do this to you, but..."

"No, no, no. I get it," he reassured me. If Joe was upset, he didn't show it.

"We have to take parenting classes, and the agency needs to conduct a home study," I explained. "So it will likely be six to nine months before the baby is placed with us. You'll have time to find another place."

"Okay. I'll start looking as soon as I get back after New Year's. Wow, talk about a Christmas present, huh?"

NO TIME LIKE THE PRESENT

Gail visited our apartment the following night. We completed the foster parent application and provided fingerprints. She warned us about the extensive paperwork and questioning involved in the home study process, which would likely take a couple of hours or more. To make the evening more enjoyable, we ordered pizza. Gail took out a pencil, a legal pad, and her home study checklist.

No question was off-limits. Our private habits, family and work histories, medical conditions, friends, affiliations, and life philosophies were all fair game. Although logistical details, such as the size and layout of our apartment were important, the home study felt more like an investigation and examination of our psychological temperaments.

"How long will everything take?" I had a few questions before she began crossing off the ones on her checklist.

"The home study will take some time to complete. But we'll do it in stages, not all at once."

"And the baby? When should we expect to get him?"

"My best guess would be around six to nine months," she said.

"So we have time to prepare," Danny said, tapping my hand.

In addition to the home study, Gail informed us about other requirements we should anticipate. These included compulsory parenting classes, future court appearances, and frequent home visits from her or other caseworkers.

"I hate to ask this," I hesitated, "but could someone object to us adopting?"

"Like who?" She asked.

"Pete's worried someone from the agency, or even the court, might undermine our efforts," Danny explained.

Gail dropped her pencil and looked over the top of her glasses, restraining a smirk. She shot me a look that said: *Are you out of your mind? Because of the judge's orders, we are doing everything we can to expedite this adoption process. Not everyone has it as easy. So just chill out.*

Instead of saying that, she provided additional information about the agency's policies, including their recent initiative of reaching out to the gay community. She assured us we had no reason to worry. Folks from Talbot Perkins even marched in the annual New York City Pride Parade.

"My parents march too," I added. "With PFLAG."

"Your parents are members of PFLAG?" Gail asked.

"Yeah, for a few years now."

"In North Jersey?" she asked.

"Yes," I confirmed.

"I think I've met them," she said. "At a meeting. I recognized your last name." Gail shared that she lived in northern Jersey with her son, who had recently come out. She had attended a PFLAG meeting to see what it was all about.

"Honestly," she shook her head in disbelief. "Tell them I said hi. Wow, what a small world."

The three of us sat around our small dining table for the next couple of hours, now scattered with paperwork and folders.

We tried not to stain the documents with pizza grease as we got deep into the questions and answers. Time flew by like we were old friends catching up after being out of touch. By around 9 pm, Danny and I had grown tired of talking about ourselves—that's all we had done for hours—so we asked Gail if we could call it a night. Thankfully, she agreed. We had accomplished a lot, but the rest would have to wait until our next session.

Later that night, Danny and I reflected on the random dots coming together before our eyes.

"What are the chances that you find a baby who is placed with an agency actively seeking gay and lesbian foster parents, and then the person conducting our home study has met my parents?"

An explanation escaped us. But as we added this new information to the other coincidences, starting with Danny being in the right place at the right time to find the baby, Karen's persistence in flipping through the white pages to find him, and the judge asking Danny to adopt—we couldn't help but get goosebumps.

Wednesday, December 20, 2000

Danny and I appeared in Family Court.

```
FAMILY COURT, STATE OF N.Y.
60 LAFAYETTE STREET, N.Y.C.
YOUR CASE HAS BEEN ADJOURNED
TO:
DATE: 12/20  TIME: 9:30 A.M.
IN PART: 6   ON: 9th  FLOOR
```

Our reminder slip

Walking in, we had no idea if Judge Cooper knew of my existence. Could I potentially be a deal breaker? What if she had aksed Danny to adopt without knowing he was gay and in a relationship? Would she take back her offer? Was it even possible for us, an unmarried gay couple, to take in a foster child or adopt?

The baby's representatives met us in the waiting area. Karen and Terri quickly briefed us on what to expect. They assured us that once inside the courtroom, all we needed to do was state our intention to adopt. Then, the judge would give further instructions and adjourn until early 2001—after the holidays—when the legal process of making us parents would begin in earnest.

"It'll be quick," Gail said.

A court official called our case number. We grabbed our coats and made our way to the courtroom.

As we entered, Judge Cooper was already seated, engrossed in reviewing and shuffling papers. It wasn't the grand entrance you see on television. There was no ceremonial announcement of "all rise for the Honorable Judge Cooper." She looked up briefly, acknowledging our presence as the next case on her docket.

Without any further ado, Judge Cooper began questioning Karen and Gail about the baby's current situation and why he was still in his current home. It became clear that the judge wanted him to be removed.

"We've begun the home study for the two gentlemen with us today," Gail said.

Judge Cooper turned her attention toward us and flashed a smile, if you can call relaxing her forehead, cheeks, and jaw a smile.

"Mr. Daniel and his partner, Mr. Peter," Gail said, "visited the baby last week."

"And how did that go, gentlemen?" Judge Cooper asked.

"Great, great," we said in unison.

"And you're here today because you want to adopt Baby Ace? I'm hoping that's why you're here," she said.

"It is," we replied.

The judge paused, taking a moment to absorb our response. Her smile widened.

After asking Karen and Gail a few more questions, Judge Cooper looked through her calendar for a moment.

"How would you like him for the holiday?" she asked.

What holiday? Memorial Day? Labor Day?

Of course, she meant Christmas—we knew that, but that was just a few days away. Our nerves were jolted and went numb at the same time.

Neither of us recalls our response—shock has a way of blurring—but we must have nodded or said something like "Sure" or "Yes" or "That's great" because the judge rattled off a litany of directives without missing a beat.

"Gentlemen," the judge said. "Will Friday work for you?"

FRIDAY? The only thing between now and then is Thursday.

She poised her pen to sign the order.

Again, I assume we made some affirmative gesture or sound. Judge Cooper scribbled her signature, then, a split second later, thanked us for being there and adjourned the hearing.

Gail was right. It was quick. In less than five minutes, Judge Cooper deduced we were ready for parenthood, induced our labor, and reduced our nine months of preparation to thirty-six hours. Outside the courtroom, the three women huddled, strategizing how to implement the judge's instructions.

"Um, what just happened?" I interjected.

"You're getting a baby for Christmas," Karen replied.

They say luck favors the prepared. We were anything but. Thirty-six hours! Time was of the essence. The clock ticked. From the moment we left the courtroom, we had thirty-five hours and fifty-nine minutes remaining, and every passing second equaled a second lost. Roaming the streets to process my emotions was not an option. Worrying seemed frivolous and indulgent, a luxury we couldn't afford. Tick. Thirty-five hours and fifty-eight minutes.

Upon arriving home, I immediately called my parents. After all, when we informed them of our adoption plans at the pizzeria, my dad had urged us to reach out if we needed anything. And now we needed everything. After an onslaught of questions—most of which we had no answer to—my parents sprang into action, rallying the entire family. That evening and the following day, my relatives mobilized like never before, scattering in all directions to brave the frenzied holiday shopping so that their new grandson, nephew, and cousin would have everything he could possibly need and more.

While they acquired blankets, bottles, diapers, and other necessities, Danny and I scoured the Barnes & Noble parenting section for an instruction manual. We sat, squatted, and clogged the aisle. We pulled out nearly every available book and organized them into piles on the floor: yes, no, or maybe. We flipped through each, scanning the pages until finally deciding to purchase *The Baby Book* and *What to Expect The First Year* and, in a nod to the future, *What to Expect The Second Year*. For the rest of the day and night, we crammed for the exam arriving the next day.

Also, that night, I called Joe in California to deliver the news that he needed to move out much sooner than any of us had expected. Like us, he had assumed we would have at least six months to change our living situation. The timeline had been drastically shortened.

I felt terrible about evicting a fellow Rookie, a teammate, and, above all, one of my closest friends. It meant subjecting him to the agonizing process of finding an affordable place to live in New York City. Plus, there was little he could do from three thousand miles away. But waiting until he returned wasn't an option. It was only fair, if fair at all, to let him know so he could at least mentally prepare.

After some small talk and asking about his flight, I got straight to the point. "I hate to do this to you," I said, "but we're bringing the baby home tomorrow..."

"What?"

"Yeah, I know. We're just as surprised."

"Petey, wow."

"So it kinda means, well, not kinda, but... I just wanted to let you know you'll have to move out when you get back."

"Oh," Joe replied, followed by a long silence, a pregnant pause in response to our short pregnancy.

"You can take Danny's apartment starting February 1st," I attempted to soften the blow. "He told the subletter he had to leave, so it's yours if you want it."

"I'll think about it, Petey."

Joe didn't dwell on the situation or his predicament. He called me back the next day.

"Petey," he said, "this is a big change for all of us. But I'm happy for you guys. And I'm relieved I don't have to look for a place to live. I'll take Danny's apartment. You know, someday we'll look back and laugh about how this kid kicked me out."

Ready or not, in less than twelve hours, Danny and I would have a baby. White knuckles on the steering wheel, we were about to enter parenthood with the wariness and unease of a first-time driver. We prayed we didn't get into an accident.

PICKING UP BABY

Friday, December 22, 2000

Danny and I hopped on the 1 train and arrived at the foster care agency at 9:15 am. Our new son wasn't there yet, but his eager grandparents were. Gail showed us to the medical station in the back—a plain, drab, powder-blue room. A tribal print and some kid-drawn art hung on the wall. The room was sparse, containing only the examination basics: a table, a chair, and a scale.

Cheryl had gone to get the baby and was due back any minute. An hour passed. While waiting, I developed a deepening case of stage fright—we'd soon be on display as parents.

Finally, we heard a voice from the hallway. "He's here!"

Danny and I reached for each other's hands, trying to steady ourselves. He looked at me with misty eyes and smiled.

"Papa and Daddy, your son is here," the nurse said as she carried him into the room. Swaddled in multiple layers from head to toe, only the baby's big brown eyes peeked through. The nurse sniffed his butt and hammed up her reaction for our benefit. "P.U.! I hate to tell you, but he's stinky. I'll remove his clothes, but you guys are doing the rest."

"Hah, welcome to parenthood," Dad said.

"Don't you have somewhere to be?" I gave him a sideways glance.

Dad was deviating from the morning schedule he had come up with. He was supposed to drop Mom off at the agency and then go straight to our apartment to meet my sister, where they would unload all the baby stuff from their cars and set up a makeshift nursery in our bedroom. Dad glanced at the clock. He was running late. He handed the video camera to Mom, practically guaranteeing we'd end up with more footage of the floor, walls, and ceiling than of Kevin.

"See you later, little guy," Dad patted his new grandson on the head on his way out.

"See this?" The nurse said with disgust. We gathered around the table. "See what they dressed him in? Rags!"

"Don't worry," Mom said. "Grandma's prepared." Ever the contingency planner, she had brought Kevin some new outfits.

The nurse stepped aside and motioned for Danny and me to take over. Danny pulled the diaper tabs. Left side, then right. Like popping open a vacuum-sealed package of poo, the fumes hit with the force of a passing garbage truck. Except this one idled right under our noses.

"Oh god, that stinks," I covered my face and stifled a gag.

"You'll get used to it," Mom said.

"Look at this," the nurse said, shaking her head in disbelief over Kevin's condition. A blistering rash covered his entire groin, from his belly button in front to his rib cage in the back. His skin was red, raw, oozing, peeling—like a third-degree burn.

Kevin's petrified stare and rigid posture said it all. With his arms clenched over his chest and his legs pulled in tight toward his stomach, he scrunched into the fetal position. Our first role as parents became clear—we needed to assure him that he was safe and establish a sense of trust and security.

Paternal instincts we didn't know we had kicked in. Danny and I gently stroked his head, arms, and legs, hoping to provide some comfort. We knew that gaining his trust would take more than just physical touch, but in that moment, our only desire was to alleviate his pain and let him know that he would no longer suffer in silence. We were here to fill the void of abandonment with abundance and transform his neglect into nourishment.

"Hey, little guy, it's going to be okay." I adjusted the brim of my baseball cap, leaned over, and kissed his forehead. Kevin's wide eyes followed my every movement, fixating on my cap's red New Jersey Devils logo. Danny lovingly ran his fingers through Kevin's wispy hair as I gently rubbed his torso. Kevin cooed, and his face lit up with a smile when I kissed his belly and made a raspberry sound.

"He likes that," Danny said.

Encouraged, I did it again.

"Is Papa being silly?" Danny asked. Kevin gurgled and smiled.

Is Papa being silly? It was the first time Danny had uttered that question, but I would hear him ask it countless times in the future. Each time, he'll ask it with the same joyful and tender inflection, brimming with wonder and gratitude for having the privilege to ask at all.

"Be gentle," Mom interjected as we cleaned around Kevin's bottom. "Wipe away from his coolie." She directed. "Lift his legs up. Make sure you get in the folds."

"Mom!" I said abruptly. I couldn't take another unsolicited instruction.

"Whaa?" she responded innocently. "Grandma's just trying to help."

Once the cleaning was done, the nurse measured Kevin's height, weight, and head circumference. For the latter, she wrapped a tape measure around his temples, sizing him for the Mets cap he'd soon be getting from his Papa. She plotted dots on a graph, connecting them with a line, then moved across the y-axis to declare, "He's a big boy. Ninety-ninth percentile." We had no clue what that meant but figured the ninety-ninth percentile was probably better and more robust than the ninth percentile.

We allowed Kevin's diaper burn to air out and cool off. He seemed to enjoy the exposure and freedom. And although he reflexively curled up again, his grip seemed less tense. Just a few minutes of affection had made a noticeable difference. He appeared more relaxed.

For the next half hour, he watched us, and we watched him. Mutual adoration. Danny and I couldn't stop smiling. Kevin remained fixated on my cap. I took it off and placed it on his head. When it swallowed his entire face, he fussed to get it off. He preferred it where he could see it, on his Papa's head.

I unfolded a fresh diaper. Danny set Kevin down on top and applied medicated cream. We pulled the leg cutouts around his hips and up to his belly but then stalled out. Fastening the diaper baffled us. Danny and I must have looked like ancient time travelers who were confused by modern technology.

"You have it backward, guys," Mom said, laughing at our ineptitude. The tabs with the Velcro go in back." With one hand on the camera, she motioned with her other hand to lift the baby and flip the diaper around. With the diaper on correctly, Danny and I moved on to the onesie. The snap buttons were slightly more manageable but still a bit tricky. It took us some time, but we eventually completed the task.

Gail returned with a folder filled with documents: hospital intake forms, the Foundling Report, and information on WIC, a supplemental nutrition program meant to promote and support good health for women, infants, and children. We could use WIC checks to buy formula, and other accepted food items.

Also in the folder was a letter on agency letterhead stating that Kevin was in our care and custody. The last item in the packet was a "getting to know your new son" information sheet.

REPORT OF FOUNDLING

NEW YORK CITY DEPT. OF HEALTH

DATE FILED: OCT -2 P 2:21

1. PLACE: NEW YORK CITY (a) Borough of Manhattan (b) Street Address: 150 William Street, NYC, NY 10038

2. Name of child or Name assigned to child (Type or Print): Baby Boy Doe aka Daniel Ace Doe

3. SEX: Male

4. Approximate Date of Birth: Month 8, Day 28, Year 00

Disposition of child: New born baby boy was discovered wrapped in a wool shirt on the floor of the West 14th St.8th Avenue Subway station in Manhattan child's unbilical cord was intact. Parentage is inconclusive.

The foundling report

"Grandma, could you come with me?" Gail asked. "I need to show you something."

Thinking Gail was about to share a secret, Mom handed over the camera and followed her. Once in the hall, Gail turned to us and winked before closing the door. Thanks to her, Papa, Daddy, and Kevin were now truly alone for the first time.

While Danny doted on our son, I read Kevin's hospital intake report from the night he was found. The report revealed that his toxicology was clean—no traces of drugs or alcohol were found in his system. However, despite being wrapped in the hoodie, the report stated that he was slightly hypothermic, a fact we had not known.

"You want to hold him?" Danny asked. I nodded, excited to bond more with our son. As I held Kevin, Danny wrapped his arm around us and squeezed my shoulder.

"And so it begins," I said.

"Yep," Danny said, "we're a family."

And responsible for keeping the little miracle in my arms alive.

Waiting to take Kevin home

FIRST NIGHT, SILENT NIGHT

We bundled Kevin and headed home.

Once outside, it began to snow. The flurries triggered a painful memory for my mom. In February 1967, a day or two after she lost her baby, there had been a big snowstorm. Mom gazed up past the drifting snowflakes to the heavens, then to Kevin, and smiled—an old agony soothed by a new joy.

We considered hailing a cab, but since Kevin had arrived via the subway, it seemed fitting to bring him home the same way. We walked toward Penn Station.

The train was mostly empty. Danny held Kevin and took a seat in the corner. Mom sat next to them. I gripped the crossbar above, standing guard for the short ride to 14th Street. A passenger next to us glanced at Kevin, then me, then Danny, then back to Kevin, and softly nodded and smiled.

As Danny slid the key into the lock outside our apartment, we heard Linda announce, "They're here!" from the other side.

"Hey, little man," Linda said while reaching to take Kevin from my arms.

"Welcome to your new home," Danny said, pulling the cover off Kevin's head so he could see more of the space. His eyes shifted in every direction to take it all in.

The apartment had been invaded. An arsenal of boxes and bags—diapers, blankets, bottles, and more—covered the futon and table. In our bedroom, a wood-slatted crib borrowed from my parents' neighbor had materialized in the corner where a small bookshelf used to be. That was now on top of our dresser. My dad and sister rearranged the room and made things fit, albeit haphazardly, in any way they could. I took a deep breath. I hoped our life, turned upside down at the moment, would settle into a manageable routine.

As a reward for his labor, Dad salivated over a Chinese takeout menu. "Hope the little guy likes chicken lo mein," he said before ordering lunch for everyone.

My parents left soon after we ate. On their way out, we received some reassurance from Mom, "You're going to be fine," and from Dad, "Call if you need anything." My sister, however, couldn't leave just yet. Kevin had snuggled himself into a nap on her. About a half-hour later, he woke, and Linda left.

We were finally alone. No caseworker, no nurse, no grandparents, no aunt. Just the three of us at home as a family unit for the first time. For a few hours, Danny and I would catch each other's dumbfounded expressions. *Is this a dream? Are we actually a family?*

Since we hadn't slept much the night before, we were both exhausted. But having just napped, Kevin was wide awake. Danny and I took turns holding him, making faces, and tickling—all the silly things adults do with babies. I carried him like a football, belly down on my forearm with his head resting in the crook of my elbow, and gave him an extended tour of his new home. We lingered at the window. Three stories up, his eyes opened wide to watch the commotion below. A giant sponge, he soaked it all in.

It wasn't long before his eyes drooped, and he was ready for another nap or to finish the one he started on my sister.

On my chest, we listened to each other's heartbeats. Sucking his thumb, he seemed so content. He soon closed his eyes and then drooled on my favorite T-shirt, marking the territory as his forever. I rubbed his back and kissed his head a million times. I took long, slow inhales to capture his scent. He looked so peaceful. Angelic.

Kevin and Papa

Danny sat on the floor next to us, propped his back against the futon cushion, and just watched. Only a fool could have passed up that moment. And I almost was that fool. Thank God for Danny's certitude, steadfastness, and, yes, his nonchalant assuredness in pushing us toward that moment.

When he woke, Kevin needed a diaper change, a bottle, and a burp. Then he needed more play time, another diaper change, a bottle, and a burp, followed by a bath, pajamas, and sleep. In other words, our new Friday night.

Everything ran as smoothly as could be until the first feeding. Since we had finished all the pre-mixed bottles the nurse gave us, we needed to prepare the formula from scratch. The info sheet stated he drank at least seven ounces, but he drank barely two ounces from the bottles we mixed. Something was wrong. We double-checked our method. One scoop of formula? Correct. Warm water? Check. What was the problem? Why wasn't he drinking? Was it his position? We propped him up. No difference. It's not like he pushed the bottle away. On the contrary, he sucked and sucked, but nothing came out. I examined the nipple.

"Maybe the hole is too small," I turned the bottle upside down and squeezed. A few drops came out. "He could suck all night and starve." Until then, neither of us had concerned ourselves with how milk flowed from a nipple. You'd think growing up on a farm with cows, Danny would've had some experience. But he hadn't milked a thing in his life. His family's cows were for burgers, not shakes.

"What should we do?" Danny asked.

I grabbed a fork and thought about stretching the hole with a tine. But what if I made it too big? We could see the headline in the next day's New York Post: FORMULA FOR DISASTER: GAYS DROWN BABY.

We ruled out a do-it-yourself job on the nipples.

I ran downstairs to the two pharmacies on opposite corners. Who knew there would be such a variety of nipples to choose from? There were cross-cut nipples, tri-vented nipples, round-top nipples, flat-top nipples, precision-flow nipples, orthodontic nipples, dripless nipples, self-adjusting nipples, latex nipples, and silicone nipples (for the natural feel). I selected one of each. The cashier stifled a laugh when I placed them on the counter.

"Stocking stuffers," I said.

Back home, I dumped the bag of nipples on the dining table. Danny tore one open and inserted it into the screw ring thingy for the bottle.

"Stop! We have to boil it first." I snatched it from his hands.

"Boil?" he asked.

"Read the instructions on back," I said.

"Put the water on," Danny chuckled, thinking he was being cute. Over the years, he had heard my dad yell, "Put the water on," to my mom when it was time for Sunday macaronis. Not knowing which nipple would work best, I put the water on and boiled one of each type. They bobbed around like latex raviolis without the gravy. Eventually, through trial and error, we found the perfect nipple that secreted just the right amount of liquid to satisfy Kevin's hunger without causing him to gag or drown.

Kevin and Daddy

Nighttime arrived fast, Kevin's first in the Vermin's luxurious honeymoon suite. Even though the books cautioned against putting a baby to sleep on his stomach, the information sheet from Gail said Kevin would not fall asleep on his back. We'd have to make our first executive decision. Better safe than sorry, we heeded the books' advice and placed him on his back, face up.

Kevin kicked and screamed bloody murder. His raw emotion, in stark contrast to the quiet, docile temperament he exhibited until then, caught us completely by surprise and was a little scary. We tried soothing him, caressing his belly and head, but our touch had no effect whatsoever. When we picked him up, he stopped. So we rocked him to sleep in our arms. Once he seemed to be out, we placed him back in the crib. But before his skin even touched the mattress, the screaming started.

How could he sleep so soundly one second and then be wide awake with lungs at full strength the next?

We repeated the process. More screaming. We figured he would tire out eventually, but he never did. After about twenty minutes of uninterrupted wailing, we turned him over. He stopped protesting instantly, like we'd flipped a switch to turn him off. Now a little smug for winning the battle, as much as an infant can emit smugness, he wiggled his head to find his thumb, put it in his mouth, sucked, and fell asleep within seconds. And he never cried again for the rest of the night. But we couldn't stop worrying about the book's warning and once again imagined a tragic news headline: GAY SIDS: DADS SUFFOCATE BABY.

For the first few hours, we sat on the floor next to the crib, listening to every breath and watching every twitch. We softly hummed Christmas carols bleeding in from the living room speakers.

One of us always stayed by the crib's side for the rest of the evening and night, obsessively checking on him. Luckily, we didn't need to travel far. The foot of our bed almost touched the edge of his crib. We would place a finger under his nose or mouth or lightly touch his chest to ensure he was breathing.

Kevin slept ten hours straight—through the clanging pipes, honking cars, screeching buses, idling trucks, and blaring ambulance sirens. We never put him on his back again.

In the morning, Kevin peered through the crib railings without making a sound, not even a whimper. He yawned, stretched, and ended with a shudder of contentment. Then his eyes widened as if to ask, "Good morning, what's for breakfast?"

We changed his diaper, fed him a bottle, and dressed him without any problems. Afterward, we placed him in the car seat—the only thing we had to put him in beside the crib or our laps—and went to the diner two doors down. Danny and I craved the sleep-deprived hangover special: greasy eggs, bacon, and stale, metallic coffee.

A server recognized us and did a double take. Without saying a word, another server paused at the edge of our table, pointed at Kevin, then at Danny and me, and made a circular motion with his finger as if to ask if Kevin was ours and if we were all together. We nodded. He gave us a spirited thumbs-up.

Danny and I still couldn't believe a baby was in the booth with us and that we were dads—his dads.

Kevin absorbed everything and studied his new life with a keen eye. In the years to come, we would learn that this was precisely the type of person he would become: curious, observant, thoughtful, and astute.

After breakfast, we packed our bags, now multiplied by the power of baby, and loaded up my beat-up cobalt blue '91 Mazda hatchback. I shouldn't have owned the car. I didn't need one in New York. But when I moved to Manhattan in '94 and put it up for sale, my parents implored me to keep it. They knew I wouldn't be able to visit them as often if I didn't have a car. "Don't sell it," Dad told me, "we'll take care of the remaining payments." The car my parents insisted I keep and helped pay for now served as a reliable grandchild visitation transport vehicle. Their investment had paid off.

We strapped Kevin in and drove to their house for the holiday weekend. Danny sat with Kevin in the back. Within minutes, our son had fallen asleep and was out for the entire trip.

Motion still lulls him into a state of deep tranquility to this day, whether by car, bus, train, plane or boat. Then and now, he has always looked like an angel when sleeping—a beacon of hope and promise we could watch for hours, and we often did.

Time more than well spent.

SHINING STAR

Mom and Dad went all out for Christmas. All their tchotchkes, knick-knacks, wreaths, banners, and figurines escaped from boxes in the attic to cover every inch of their house, inside and out, right down to the doorknobs. They slathered decorations on their four-foot, tabletop artificial tree—its green bristles barely visible behind the red ribbons, bows, and gold ornaments. Loaded up to the last needle, it's a wonder the tree didn't collapse. Underneath, a rustic nativity scene waited to be surrounded by their vintage, yet anachronistic, electric train set.

"Peter, the trains, the village," Mom would say, "Let's go. Chop, chop." Building the tracks and her Dickens Village were still my responsibility. New father or not, it had to get done. Mom had been collecting Dickens pieces for over twenty years. She had so many that displaying all of them would take over the entire house. My job was to edit and curate the collection. First, I'd line up all the boxes of miniature Victorian buildings and cottages on the floor to decide which ones would get displayed. Then, like a Saks window designer, I constructed the Village scene and aesthetic. My favorite, Scrooge's house, and Mom's favorite, the Brick Abbey, always made the cut.

Mom also collected the annual gold-plated ornament from the Danbury Mint. In 2000, the ornament depicted the town of Bethlehem with a big gold star dangling over the city. Friends and neighbors must have seen the light illuminating my parent's house and followed the star to visit the miraculous subway baby. Folks were in and out all day to catch a glimpse of Kevin. And everyone had a gift. Stuffed animals, blankets, clothes, and toys—anything a new baby could want or need, except frankincense and myrrh.

Kevin became the center of everyone's attention, the focal point in my parents' cramped living room. In return, Kevin made everyone else the focus of his attention. On his stomach, to get a better view of his admirers, he pushed up and strained to observe the comings and goings. When on his side or back, which he tolerated only while awake, he still clenched his arms across his chest and tucked in his legs.

I made it my mission to help him relax and uncurl from the fetal position. I would grab his chunky calves, make cycling motions, and pretend he kicked me. I called this game "Kickboxing Baby," and Kevin and I played it all day. He laughed heartily every time he connected and landed a foot in my face to score a point.

Kickboxing Baby and Papa

While Kickboxing Baby relaxed his legs, his upper body required a different technique. For that, I raised and spread his arms over his head in an elongated stretch. "One, two, three," I pinned his arms up and scored points by kissing his belly, cheeks, and head, eliciting more giggles. His eyes twinkled with delight. I hoped that using physical therapy through loving play would allow him to feel safe enough to release his protective clutch and open up. And for the most part, it worked. By the end of the day, Kevin's guard came down, just in time for a rite of passage—a bath by Grandma.

My mom lined the kitchen sink with towels, filled it with warm water, and plopped him in. She had performed this ritual, a baptism of sorts, with her first two grandkids. Number three, Kevin, would not escape Grandma's sink bath. Propped up against the side of the basin like an oversized macaroni pot, he furrowed his brows and watched his grandma rub a mildly soapy washcloth under his armpits, over his belly, then down each arm and leg. Based on his bug-eyed reaction, we assumed he didn't know what to make of the bath and Grandma's singing. We could only imagine his thoughts: "This is nuts," "That feels good," and "Oh, you missed a spot."

On the night of December 23rd, Danny, Kevin, and I slept in my parents' musty basement. Kevin was out cold the second his head hit the bottom of a neighbor's borrowed "pack 'n play." While he seemed to sleep comfortably wherever he was, Danny and I tossed and turned all night on the lumpy pullout sofa bed.

Kevin met the rest of his aunts, uncles, and cousins on my side of the family the following night, Christmas Eve. As far as Italian families go, ours was unusually small. Mom was an only child. Dad had one sister. My parents had aimed for a big family—at least six kids who would go on to have lots of grandkids—a future filled with youthful energy. But things didn't quite work out that way. They ended up having five and losing one.

In addition, my younger brother Matthew and I turned out to be gay, making it unlikely that we would be sources for grandchildren. At the time, Linda was childless and unsure about having kids. Until that Christmas, my older brother Joseph's boys were my parents' only grandkids. The large clan they had hoped for ended up being less Italian and more Asian, less straight and more gay, and less energetic and more serene than they ever could have predicted. Despite having to adjust their expectations in terms of size and composition, they loved their modern family with all their hearts.

As for our Christmas Eve meal, my family bucked the tradition of eating fish. Growing up, none of us ate sea creatures. So instead of eating a feast of seven fishes, we ate the yeast of leaven dishes: pizzas, calzones, and zeppoles. Mom and Dad prepared the dough days ahead of time, mixing and kneading it in huge aluminum pots. They covered the pots with dish towels and stored them in the basement near the furnace. Dad swore the dry heat "helped the dough rise nice." They warned us to steer clear and "don't even think about touching or peeking under the towels." And if, for some reason, we needed to be in the basement, we had better tiptoe.

Once the dough had risen, it was divided for its different uses. Mom rolled and flattened it for pizza crusts and calzones. Dad heated oil in the deep fryer, which was only used once a year, and cooked test batches of zeppoles until they were golden brown and crispy. Their house smelled like a greasy, tomato-y, doughy, and sugary emporium in late December. Dad placed the fried zeppoles on brown grocery bags that blanketed the counter. Like a vulture circling its prey, I'd wait for him to turn back to the deep fryer, then swoop in to capture the runt of the litter and gobble it up. Even without powdered sugar, Dad's zeppoles tasted like greased lightning. Hot and crunchy, the first bite oozed with oil until your teeth punctured the firm yet gooey center. It was like eating a piece of heaven, and it always made me high. Dad manned the fryer all day, always making enough to share with friends and neighbors.

On Christmas Eve, everyone in the family wanted to hold and keep Kevin in their arms, none more than Christian, my five-year-old nephew and Kevin's new cousin. When it was time for Kevin to eat, Christian wedged himself in the corner of the sofa, propped up pillows, and begged to feed him, which he did with both hands and one huge proud smile.

His brother Daniel, two years older, had practical concerns.

"Uncle Pete," he asked, "what's he going to call you?"

"What do you mean?"

"Are you both going to be Daddy?"

"Well, since my name starts with P and Danny's starts with D, I'll be Papa, and he'll be Daddy." This answer satisfied Daniel for the moment, but the cogs kept turning in his head, and he soon had another question.

"Did Danny really find him in the subway?" he asked.

"Yes, he did."

"And now he's yours?"

"Yep."

"Why?" he asked.

"Because we want him to be a part of our family."

I didn't want to go into too much detail. Besides, truthfully, I couldn't articulate a reason beyond that. Much of the past week, from our court appearance to bringing Kevin home to that moment with Daniel, remained beyond my comprehension.

All the commotion wore Kevin out, and he fell asleep around 9 pm. After everyone else left, we helped my parents clean up. Danny dried dishes with Mom in the kitchen while I rearranged the dining room with Dad. Sometime between removing the table leaves and pushing the ends back together, Dad asked if we had thought about having Kevin baptized. *Wait, hadn't Mom already taken care of that in the sink?*

Baptism was of significant importance to my parents for three reasons. First, it was a customary practice in the Roman Catholic tradition. Second, it provided insurance. Should anything happen to Kevin before he was baptized, his soul wouldn't be guaranteed a place in heaven. And third, they wanted to throw a christening party, inviting friends and relatives. Before we could respond, they sweetened the deal by mentioning the possibility of receiving gifts, mainly checks, and cash, to help us start our lives as a family. "You know them," Dad said, referring to his relatives, "they're not going to give you anything without a party."

Danny and I hadn't discussed how to deal with questions of religion. However, given that he was raised Southern Baptist and I was raised Roman Catholic, the subject was bound to come up, as it did that holy night.

When I looked to Danny for a reaction, he raised his eyebrows and made a face that conveyed one interpretation: These are your parents; I'll let you handle it. In that moment, no words exchanged, we silently agreed on the newly formed Stewart-Mercurio doctrine: I would deal with my parents. He would deal with his. Front and center, my parents were up first.

"No, Dad," I responded, "we haven't thought about it."

"Oh," he said, "I don't mean for you to do it now. You know, later, when the weather's warmer. In the spring."

"I'm not sure we can," I explained. "Technically, he's still a ward of the state. We don't have the authority to make those kinds of decisions for him."

I had no idea if that was true. I said it to buy Danny and me some time to discuss the matter later so we could be on the same page and present a unified response whenever the topic arose again.

"Well, can you find out from the agency?" Dad asked.

"Because if we're going to have a party," Mom said, "we need to start planning for it now."

Just what kind of party did she have in mind? Did she think I would participate in an extravagant Italian wedding-style christening affair with a raucous DJ who made us dance the Electric Slide beneath a disco ball with our baby? Well, she had better fuggedaboutit.

Sure, Danny and I could have gone along with it, baptized Kevin, and let them host a party. What harm would it have done? A splash of water on his head, and we'd collect envelopes filled with cash and checks. We did need the money, but at what cost? Had my parents carefully considered the implications? At best, I was a lapsed Catholic, if one at all. I hadn't attended Sunday mass in almost sixteen years. Would I even be welcome in a church? Would a priest agree to baptize a baby with two dads? And if so, would one of us have to stand on the sidelines of the altar and watch?

I couldn't string my parents along or give them false hope. I needed to nip the idea in the bud right then and there.

"There will be no party," I asserted. "We haven't considered it because it's not going to happen. We're not having him baptized, now or later."

"Okay," Dad said, "we're just offering, putting it out there. Something to think about."

"We appreciate the offer…" Danny acknowledged.

"But it's not going to happen," I said with finality. And that ended it. The topic never came up again.

It wasn't that night, but eventually, Danny and I did discuss the matter of religion, our personal beliefs, and our extended families. We believed Kevin's presence in our life was a transcendent, if not an outright religious, experience. However, neither of us felt the need to impose a set of religious beliefs—rigid, reformed, or otherwise—on him the way they had been imposed on us. Kevin represented the purest incarnation of divinity and godliness we had ever known, and we didn't want to sully that with dogma.

Nonetheless, we understood that religion played a significant role in Kevin's grandparents' lives, particularly through church attendance. And we wanted him to understand that part of their identity as people of faith. Since neither of us had close relationships with our own grandparents, it was important to us that Kevin did. Therefore, we decided early on that my parents could take him to a Roman Catholic Church in New Jersey, and Danny's parents could take him to a Southern Baptist Church in Texas.

The next night, on Christmas, after all the presents had been unwrapped, everyone met and held Kevin, and all the food was eaten. Danny and I loaded up the Mazda. We repeatedly packed and unpacked the trunk and backseat to make more space for everything we received. A new baby, especially one showered with Christmas gifts, doesn't travel lightly. Eventually, we crammed in only the supplies and gifts our new family would need. The rest we left with my parents.

But not the gold ornament of Bethlehem.

That came home with us.

And so did the shining star.

NO RETURNS

Tuesday, December 26, 2000

We were pretty sure Kevin had to go back to the foster care agency the day after Christmas, and he would most likely be placed back with the Garcias. I woke up that morning determined to somehow prevent that from happening. While we had no legal authority to keep Kevin, I had no plans to return him voluntarily.

"I'll let you know what happens," I told Danny before he left for work.

Alone with Kevin for the first time, the morning routine of feeding, burping, changing his diaper, and getting him dressed felt natural, as if I had been doing it for months, not just a few days. And Kevin seemed so content in his new home. He smiled more, let his guard down, relaxed, and trusted that we would care for him. To the best of an infant's ability, he expressed relief. The morning alone with my son went off without a hitch.

I didn't reach out to Gail or anyone else at the agency. I worried that keeping Kevin could jeopardize our chances of permanently keeping him. Since I hadn't heard from Gail, I hoped she had forgotten, and I wasn't about to remind her. Kevin and I enjoyed the rest of the day together, bonding as Papa and son, playing with toys on the floor, sharing kisses, and giving each other plenty of affection. Feeling a bit envious, Danny came home early to join in the fun.

The next morning, Gail called.

"You were supposed to bring the baby back yesterday," she said.

"Yesterday?" I replied. "The judge said we could have him for the holidays. We assumed that meant until after New Year's."

"We haven't received clearance from Albany," she explained. "He can't stay with you until your fingerprints are cleared."

The thought of Kevin going back to a neglectful situation broke my heart, especially after seeing how much progress he was making. I pretended I didn't know we had to return him. As far as I was concerned, Kevin wasn't going back. If Gail, the agency, the court, or the state demanded his return, they'd have to pry him from my arms.

Despite lacking any legal standing, I presented our case.

"His rash is nearly gone," I started my plea. "He's opened up. He laughs and giggles a lot. He no longer clenches his arms over his chest." Gail remained silent on the other end of the line, but I sensed her agreement. I continued, desperate to convince her. "You know as well as I do that sending him back won't be good for him. He's healing from the physical and emotional trauma. If he goes back, all of his progress will be lost. How will he ever learn to trust again? Please, there must be some way he can stay with us."

She let out a lengthy sigh and said, "I'll see what I can do."

"Thank you, Gail."

"He can stay one more night, but that's it." Another sigh indicated that she was bending the rules for us.

Unfortunately, she was constrained by the law. Suppose something terrible happened to Kevin while in our care; Gail would bear the responsibility. And yet, it was all but certain that something awful would happen if he were sent back to the Garcias.

She didn't call the next day or the day after that, but I anticipated a knock on our door at any minute. Even though our situation was wildly different, images from earlier in the year when federal agents seized Elian Gonzalez to return him to Cuba were fresh in my mind.

Tuesday turned into Wednesday, and Wednesday turned into Thursday. Gail never came. We finally heard from her on Friday, a week after picking Kevin up from the agency.

"I have some good news," she said. "Your fingerprints and background check have been processed through the State Central Registry in Albany."

"Yeah, so what does that mean?" I asked.

"It means you're cleared," she said. "He can stay with you. We can conduct the home study while he's in your custody."

I breathed a sigh of relief and called Danny to share the good news.

Kevin was home. With us. Forever.

Our clearance wasn't the only gift we received that day. A care package from Danny's mom arrived: a box sealed in seven layers of packing tape. Under all the tape and cardboard was a red, white, and blue quilt. Despite her conviction that Kevin needed both a mother and a father, she also wanted him to be warm (and patriotic). Tucked under the quilt were containers of homemade hot cocoa mix and peanut brittle, a children's picture book Bible, and a video of the biblical story of Daniel, the closest she could get, absent a Book of Kevin.

* * *

What a difference a year makes. At the end of 1999, the Y2K computer virus had the media and, hence, the entire world on edge. Could vital computer systems shut down? Would planes fall out of the sky? Bank accounts get wiped out? Nuclear missiles erroneously launched? Armageddon-like catastrophe, we were told and some believed, could very well strike at the stroke of midnight.

Just in case, Danny and I threw a big party to usher in 2000. The dawning of the new millennium occurred once in a lifetime, and only if you happened to be living at the time, which we were, so it demanded our full-throttled participation and inebriation. If the fatalistic paranoia about the Y2K virus proved correct, at least we'd have already been embalmed. We counted down to midnight for as many time zones as we could and celebrated every hour with tequila shots until finally collapsing around 4:30 am.

Whenever we remember that night, we recall it as our last hurrah before becoming parents. We also think about what else may have been going on that night and the possibility of Kevin being conceived. Maybe somewhere, two strangers to us created the boy who would become our son. Because almost nine months later, he entered our lives.

We have often wondered about the identities of these individuals and how they were connected. Was Kevin conceived by two consenting adults in the heat of passion? Or by young lovers on a fling? Or perhaps by intoxicated revelers who, like us, could barely remember what they did on New Year's Eve? We may never know. What we know is this: our paths intersected in late August, and a life was exchanged at a damp, dim subway station in Chelsea.

As timekeeping sticklers like to point out, the new millennium began at midnight of 2001, not midnight of 2000. Therefore, our celebration and that of the entire world were a year ahead of schedule. The actual new millennium began in a much different manner for us. For starters, we remained completely sober. We ate dinner, washed dishes, and bathed Kevin. We read bedtime stories and softly sang lullabies over his crib until our little boy drifted asleep. Danny and I melted into the sofa, turned on Dick Clark, but conked out by 10:30 pm, missing the ceremonial ball drop in Times Square.

The next day, we awoke early to a new era. *2001: A Baby Odyssey* now played on the big screen of our lives.

Of course, all of the hype and hysteria about Y2K turned out to be just that—hype and hysteria. The earth kept spinning and revolving around the sun. The meaning of the Y2K acronym would ultimately become nothing more than an answer to a future trivia question. But for us, it took on a whole new definition. Y2K would change from Year 2000 to Year to Kevin, hysteria to hope, virus to cure.

There was no going back.

No return to a pre-2K era.

CHILD CARE

Even though Talbot Perkins' information sheet succinctly documented Kevin's eating and sleeping habits, it still wasn't detailed and comprehensive enough for me. So I created a daily log of fill-in sheets to keep track of all his daily activities, from bodily functions to playtime. We logged each event as if Kevin's life depended on it. Filling out the forms became habitual, something we did without thinking. It comforted us to know our son was doing normal baby things.

Besides, we were told to pay attention to his diapers because the clues to his health were hidden inside. We tracked how much he ate and drank, how long he napped, how many times he peed and pooped, and noted the texture, color, and consistency of each one. If by chance a nurse, doctor, or anyone else asked, we could refer to our daily logs and reliably report, for example, that on December 29, 2000, at 1:16 pm, Kevin's diaper contained a normal volume of pale-yellow pee.

Danny and I never discussed our roles for taking care of and raising a baby. Since we had no time to figure it out beforehand, we both did everything. Over time, a natural pattern developed where we alternated diaper changes, feedings, and all the other household and baby-related responsibilities. As two men, we weren't bound by traditional mother/father roles. Who was more like a stereotypical mother? Both. Who was more like a father? Both. The trappings of a "women do this, men do that" mindset didn't apply to us. Unbound by social norms and expectations, we developed our own parenting styles, ignored the paint-by-numbers parent template, and colored outside the lines. I don't recall us arguing about any of the roles and responsibilities. If we did, they never turned into a protracted battle. At least not one worth remembering. It took about a week or two from when Kevin came home to naturally settle into attending to the tasks that matched our strengths, weaknesses, skills, and comfort levels.

Sample log by neurotic parents getting to know their new son.

Our biggest challenge was finding daycare. While my employer had given me parental leave (paid and unpaid) for a few weeks, they expected me back in the office on February 1st. That gave us most of January to find quality, affordable child care. Which, we discovered, didn't exist in New York City. We could have quality, or we could have affordable, but not both.

I opened a spreadsheet to create our first family budget, aiming to identify areas where we could reduce expenses and improve our financial situation. At the time, we only had a few hundred dollars in savings and were carrying a little over three thousand dollars in credit card debt. Additionally, Danny still had ten years left to pay off his student loans. Surprisingly, Danny and I never argued about money. There wasn't any to fight over. We could have disagreed about how to pay off our debt, but we didn't do that either. The spreadsheet dictated that we had to live frugally, paycheck to paycheck, and manage our modest means. Quality was out. Affordable was in.

A friend suggested we check out the *Irish Echo*, a newspaper which catered to individuals seeking and offering nanny services. Though unfamiliar with the newspaper, we decided to give it a shot. We circled a few ads and discussed them over dinner one evening in early January. As an experiment, we selected one ad and arranged to interview the applicant the following day.

The next day, a young woman arrived wearing a skimpy, form-fitting dress and high heels. Her platinum blonde hairdo, heavy makeup, and bright red lipstick gave her a rather dramatic appearance. While we didn't want our first impressions of her fashion choices to dictate our decision, we couldn't help but wonder if her appearance would be suitable for taking care of Kevin. We invited her inside, but she remained on the doormat.

"I can work start tomorrow possible as soon as," she said in a thick Russian accent before we even asked a question.

I wanted to say, "Thank you for coming," but I found myself mulling over the balance between quality and affordability and ended up inquiring about her rate instead. Her rate was so high that I thought she was joking and had to stifle a laugh. Unfortunately, she was completely serious. Her monthly fee exceeded our monthly rent. If she thought we could pay that kind of money, then "we wrong tree she bark up."

After an uncomfortable five minutes, we politely thanked her for coming and ended the interview. Once she had left, Danny and I exchanged skeptical glances, each of us silently thinking, "How on earth are we going to find affordable childcare?" I glanced at the other ads we had circled in the *Irish Echo*, but after that demoralizing encounter, we had little faith in finding the right person through the newspaper. Fortunately, we had a backup plan and some support to rely on. My parents, my sister, and our friend Chuck had all expressed their willingness and availability to help with childcare if needed.

One day in early January, Danny casually mentioned our predicament to a coworker. Without hesitation, she recommended Dottie, who ran a family daycare business in her apartment. His coworker's daughter had attended this daycare, and she had nothing but praise for it.

Feeling hopeful, Danny and I decided to give Dottie a call the next day.

"I'm full," she said. I can't take any more kids, but you're free to come by and take a look if you want." Despite not having any spots available for Kevin, we went anyway. It would give us some idea of how a family daycare facility operates.

When we arrived, Dottie was in the middle of preparing lunch. The aroma and humidity, reminiscent of a steam room filled with boiled fruits and veggies, instantly hit your senses. She proudly stated that her kids didn't eat jarred or canned foods. She made everything from scratch: applesauce, mashed green beans, carrots, and sweet potatoes.

Dottie led us down a short, narrow hallway cluttered with hanging coats and diaper bags and then around a corner to her tiny studio apartment's main and only room. At best, the space was 250 square feet. Five kids, a pug named Sadie and a boxer named Boo-Boo, were scattered on the floor like rugrats. "I know it's small, but the good thing is I'm always within arm's reach of any of them."

In her early sixties, Dottie was peppy and energetic. She cared deeply about the kids and treated each one as if they were her own. We were instantly drawn to her no-nonsense, attentive, loving, and warm grandmotherly style. Being there felt like being home.

"I can only have five at once and a maximum of three under the age of two," she said while checking the pot on the stove. "How old is your son?"

"A little over four months," Danny said.

"Yeah, I'm full with kids that age. It's a shame he's not older. I have a two-year-old leaving next month… So how did you guys get him?" Her directness startled us. "Surrogacy? Adoption?"

"We're going to adopt," Danny said. "Right now, he's our foster child."

"I don't know if you remember hearing about a baby that was abandoned at the subway station down the block…" I began before she interrupted.

"Last summer! How could I forget? It was all over the news. I don't understand how anybody could do that! Crazy people in this world. I've been thinking about that baby ever since."

"Well," I said, "Danny's the person who found him, and now he's our son."

Dottie tilted her head and studied our faces.

"It's true," Danny said.

"I believe you," Dottie said, still squinting her eyes. "I'm just in shock. It's so amazing. So beautiful." However, even after we told her the entire story, it wasn't beautiful enough to make room for Kevin. "I can't do it, guys. They'll shut me down."

Although we knew before going that Dottie didn't have an opening for Kevin, meeting her and seeing how she cared for her kids made us feel a profound sense of loss. It was as if we were missing out on something extraordinary that we wouldn't find elsewhere. On the bright side, we now knew the type of childcare we wanted for our son. If we couldn't have Dottie, we'd have to spend the next two weeks searching for someone just like her.

The next day, before we could begin the search, Dottie called.

"Listen, guys," she said, "I don't know if this could work or if you're even interested, but I may have a part-time opening." She explained that another family, who paid for a full-time spot, only sent their son for two or three days a week. Dottie had never offered part-time care before, but she was willing to make an exception for us—or perhaps more accurately, for the miracle subway baby.

"So I could do two days, maybe three," she said. "But only on the days when the other family isn't here."

"We'll take it," I said. It was a win-win-win for us, Dottie, and the other family, who would now pay less. Her decision to split a full-time slot had saved us just in the nick of time. There was just one more childcare issue to resolve. Since Danny and I worked late on Thursdays, past Dottie's closing time, we needed to find someone to pick up Kevin and take him home. Chuck immediately volunteered. Thursday nights became Nanny Chuck nights. Starting the following week and continuing every Thursday for the next twelve years, Chuck picked up Kevin. He fed, played, bathed, read stories, and tucked him into bed. He gave Danny and me the best gift we have ever received—a regular date night for us to spend time alone and do whatever we wanted, our weekly reminder of why we fell in love in the first place.

It's clichéd by now, but it truly does take a village. Chuck wasn't the only person we relied on. Our list of babysitters included Joe, about a third of the Rookies, bowling teammates, coworkers, and theatre friends. One night, after returning home from our date, we found Dean there with Chuck.

Dean stood by the window, holding Kevin, and looked down at Seventh Avenue.

"This is your front yard, little man," Dean said with wonder. "Some playground."

CABIN FEVER

    I never anticipated the hardest part of being a new parent would hit me so fast. Becoming parents smack-dab in the middle of the holidays didn't allow us to see how a baby would affect our day-to-day routine, but a dark, cold, snowy January certainly did. The mere thought of dressing Kevin, packing a diaper bag, preparing a bottle, and then carrying him and his posse of equipment in the stroller up and down three flights of stairs left me exhausted. Every day, I woke up and foolishly thought, "I'll write while Kevin naps." But I couldn't. The pen wouldn't move. I even stopped attending my Wednesday afternoon playwrights group. My life boiled down to feedings, diaper changes, and the in-between hours of feeling trapped. I had staring contests with Kevin's cabal of stuffed animals. That was pointless. You can't win. They never blink.

    I remembered my mom and others saying about dirty diapers, "He's your son. You'll get used to it." All lies. I never "got used to it." Changing Kevin's diaper almost always triggered a gag reflex. To mask the smell, I kept scented candles, linen spray, candy, deodorant, or magazine cologne ads nearby. This cracked Danny (and me) up, which wasn't good because laughing only leads to taking deep breaths. And I wanted to avoid doing that around a full diaper.

"You have it easy," my mom would say. "There was no such thing as disposable diapers when you were a baby. We had cloth diapers and washed them by hand." Good for you, I'd think. Extra points for getting your hands dirty.

I paced the apartment a lot that January and noticed every flaw—cracked paint, hissing pipes, and leaky faucets. Other than Danny, some days, I never spoke to another adult. I'd call him several times a day to tell him I was going crazy and couldn't handle being a stay-at-home parent. "It'll get better," he'd say, trying to soothe. He felt helpless and somewhat guilty. He had pushed us to become parents, which now affected me more than him. Danny focused on our future, assuring me I'd adjust and everything would be fine. He was right, of course, but I couldn't see past my feelings at the time.

Now, here's the odd thing about that first month home alone with Kevin: even though I felt trapped, moody, restless, and inept, with each passing day, I fell deeper in love with my son. And the last thing I wanted was for him to absorb any of my angst.

"Give it to me," Danny once said. "It's better if you unload on me than Kevin." And I often did. Danny calmly absorbed it all and never wrung it out.

In late January, we decided to change up our living situation. If the walls felt like they were closing in, then we would just take one down. The partition in the living room had to go.

Friday, February 2, 2001

I dropped Kevin off at my parents' house, borrowed some power tools from my dad, and headed back home to prepare for our do-it-yourself demolition job.

I took the first swing with the sledgehammer, and Danny took the second. Plasterboard dust filled the room. Without face masks, we inhaled the particles. Regardless, we hammered away, only to discover that the partition was more than just a simple room divider. It was incredibly well-constructed and reinforced with enormous bolts. Vertical wood beams, positioned every six inches, caused the sledgehammer to recoil when we hit them. We were woefully unprepared and in over our heads. But with a partially destroyed wall in the middle of our living room, it was too late to turn back. So we lumbered on for the rest of the day and into the night. At 10 pm, our downstairs neighbor had had enough of the drilling, banging, and sawing. They stopped me in the hallway as I dragged an overstuffed and sooty contractor garbage bag to the basement. I apologized and promised that we would stop by 11 o'clock.

On Sunday morning, we picked up where we had left off. Around noon, Maria, the building superintendent, knocked on our door. Although she lived in a different building around the corner, she would randomly swing by our building to asphyxiate the common areas with an ammonia-soaked mop. She anointed the hallway that Sunday and followed the trail of dust from the basement to our apartment. I cautiously opened the door, just a crack, to prevent her from seeing inside.

"We're building something for the baby," I said sheepishly.

Maria glanced at my dirty sweatpants and then studied the forced smile on my face. She could have ordered us to stop, as technically, we needed permission from the owner, whom we didn't even know, to make structural changes to the apartment. But we didn't see what we were doing as a modification. We considered it a restoration. A previous tenant had built the wall without the owner's knowledge, and in our view, we were simply returning the space to its original layout.

"Ay, si, si," Maria nodded. She probably knew I was lying but didn't ask to come in or press the issue. She had a "see no evil, hear no evil, speak no evil" policy. With a polite smile, she asked us to take all the bags we had brought to the basement and place them on the curb for pickup the next day.

The second part of the restoration stretched into the following week. While Kevin napped, I patched holes and sanded. The home improvement tasks kept me busy and improved my mood. The following weekend, we left Kevin with my parents again so we could paint.

Chuck came over to help, and it felt like old times in the theatre when we would order pizza and paint the set while singing along to his favorite 70s disco songs and my favorite 80s new wave hits. As we primed the walls, he told me about his new play, *We Were There,* and how he hoped Other Side would produce it by the end of the year. I freaked out but didn't let it show. How could I do that? I was committed to another production. *The Kevin Show* had just loaded in for an open-ended run. But Chuck had worked hard on the company's first two productions, both plays I had written, and I couldn't let him down. I agreed to do everything possible to bring his baby to life and ensure its success. It was the least I could do for him. We organized a reading and embarked on raising funds for the production. Although we couldn't get the show off the ground in 2001, we eventually staged *We Were There* in 2002.

Around the same time, in early 2001, our friends Roy and Greg offered to host a baby shower for us. They had recently moved from Chelsea to a charming colonial stone house in Tarrytown and said their new home was the perfect setting to celebrate the arrival of our son, Kevin. Most of our friends and family had never personally known gay parents before and wanted to commemorate not just our family but also the progress of society as a whole.

Roy and Greg assured us they would make all the arrangements: sending out invitations, managing RSVPs, and even arranging transportation for our city-dwelling friends without cars. All we needed to do was provide a guest list, create a baby registry, and show up. Once word got out, others enlisted to help, including Bruce, one of Danny's former coworkers from GMHC, his partner Henri, and of course, my mom.

But there was one problem: we didn't need anything. All of our baby-raising needs were met over the holidays, and we were fully equipped. When Danny mentioned this to Roy, he suggested turning the shower into a family-focused celebration and advised us to include items for Kevin and our home on the registry.

The idea of a family shower felt weird, but we did need to update our worn-out kitchen utensils and appliances. A blender or toaster, which we didn't have at all, would be nice. So our baby shower gradually morphed into something resembling a bridal shower, minus the bride.

Since our family dynamic was completely unconventional, we decided it was acceptable to include things like measuring cups, spatulas, pots, pans, a toaster, a blender, a decorative wall clock, and a pair of adult-sized rubber-soled house shoes on our "baby" registry. "I wouldn't want to slip," I joked, "while checking the time and counting the seconds until Kevin's toast popped."

> October 24, 1947 - Kevin Kline
> January 18, 1955 - Kevin Costner
> July 8, 1958 - Kevin Bacon
>
> August 28, 2000 - Kevin Stewart-Mercurio
>
> The most recent addition to our constellation of stars is the newest member of the Peter Mercurio, Daniel Stewart family. We would like to help our friends celebrate this heavenly arrival with a baby shower on Saturday March 10th, 2001 at 6:00 in the evening

The shower invitation

A week before the shower, Kevin developed a high fever, a wet cough, and heavy congestion. As we learned on the job, a baby doesn't know how to blow their nose. Kevin's booger-packed nostrils gave me a new favorite activity: aspirating mucus from his nose. But no matter how much or how often I aspirated, Kevin's condition didn't improve. So we took him to the doctor at Talbot Perkins. After checking his vitals, she didn't seem too concerned. She explained that babies catch colds, and this was just a bad one that needed to run its course. To help reduce his fever, she prescribed alternating doses of infant Tylenol and Advil.

Saturday, March 10, 2001

A mix of family, friends, and coworkers trekked to Tarrytown to welcome Kevin into our tribe, our village. Like he was at Christmas, Kevin was passed around from person to person. Feverish, he felt like an actual hot potato. While Danny and I mingled, Linda and Chuck kept a watchful eye on our boy.

Dean grabbed my arm early in the evening and pulled me aside for a warm hug.

"It's a beautiful thing you boys have done for this baby," he said.

"I'm glad you're here," I said.

"I wouldn't have missed this for the world, Petey. Look, I rarely admit when I'm wrong, but I was wrong. You and Danny are the best thing that's ever happened for this kid, and he's the best thing that's ever happened for you. I was scared for you. I still am. But what do I know? I'm just a lil' ol' guy from Louisiana. I don't know nothin' about all this baby stuff."

Dean, the once lone dissident, had come around. And it meant the world to me to have his blessing and support.

"Let me hold that little slugger," my softball teammate Oscar reached for Kevin. None of us would have been there if it hadn't been for Oscar introducing Danny and me. A proud papa himself, he took pride knowing he was partly responsible for us being a family.

"He's really hot," Oscar said. "Muy Caliente."

Overhearing the comments about Kevin's temperature, Chuck alerted my sister. Together, they wrangled Kevin from Oscar and whisked him away to a bedroom upstairs. Chuck then came back down to get my mom. She went to check on Kevin and immediately sent Chuck back down to get us. Danny and I were mingling with guests in the kitchen when he gestured for our attention. His forehead glistened from the three trips up the staircase.

"Kevin's with your mom and sister upstairs," he said. "You guys need to go up." Danny and I went immediately.

"He has a 103.5 fever," Mom said as we entered the bedroom. "I don't like how he's breathing. Look at his chest. It's labored. He's struggling to take in air."

Kevin's condition was rapidly deteriorating. We didn't know what to do.

"Let's ask Nicholas to look at him," Danny suggested.

Nicholas was the only doctor in the house. Though not a pediatrician, we were confident he'd know what to do. Chuck left to get him, making it his fourth trip up and down the stairs. Nicholas gently touched Kevin's head, neck, and chest, instructing us to keep him as cool as possible. He advised against using heavy pajamas, sheets, blankets, or quilts. Initially, he didn't seem alarmed, but then he suggested we take Kevin to the pediatrician first thing on Monday.

My dad popped his head in to say that some guests needed to leave to catch a train back to the city, but they were waiting for us to open presents. At that moment, the last thing we wanted to do was unwrap gifts. With our son burning up, we would have preferred to let the party naturally come to an end and send everyone home without the spectacle. But even on an unconventional occasion, there is tradition. Everyone was there for us. And the show must go on.

So, we put on happy faces, graciously opened cards and gifts, and, in true shower tradition, even stuck bows and ribbons on our heads. Meanwhile, our three nurses—Mom, Linda, and Chuck—took turns caring for Kevin. Eventually, the gift unwrapping ended, trains were caught, and the shower curtain finally fell. Unfortunately, the same could not be said about Kevin's fever. That didn't budge.

It only got worse.

A lot worse.

SOMETHING SPECIAL

The next day, a Sunday, Kevin's fever spiked to over 104 degrees and didn't break. Since we had plans to take him to the doctor at the foster care agency on Monday afternoon, Danny and I did our best to comfort him until then. One of us sat on the floor next to his crib all night, monitoring him until dawn.

Danny went to work early the next day so he could go with me to the agency. I tried feeding Kevin a bottle. He drank less than an ounce. I wished he could talk and tell me how he was feeling. Instead, I relied on his nonverbal cues and instinct. My gut feeling told me we couldn't wait until our appointment at the agency. I called Gail and described his condition, which seemed to be getting worse by the second.

"Don't come here," she said. "Take him to the medical clinic across from St. Vincent's right now." I hastily packed a diaper bag, shoved it in the fold of the stroller, slung it over my shoulder, and carried Kevin to the clinic.

Upon arrival, I checked in at the front desk then sat in the waiting area. I kissed Kevin's head and gently caressed his cheeks. He was burning up. Kevin began to fuss in my arms, so I transferred him to the stroller and lightly rocked it. Apart from his short, rapid gasps for air, he lay motionless with his eyes closed.

I called my sister, Linda, for support. She happened to be meeting a friend uptown, but when she heard about Kevin, she left her friend and headed downtown to join us.

I watched the clock. Thirty minutes passed. Then an hour. Kevin's condition continued to deteriorate. Each gasp he took seemed like it could be his last. I checked with the front desk to make sure we hadn't been forgotten. They assured me that they were just busy. Monday mornings were the busiest time to see a doctor at this clinic, as anyone who had survived the weekend with an ailment sought treatment as soon as the doors opened. For over an hour, I watched and listened to a nurse call out dozens of names until, finally, nearing the two-hour mark, she looked at her clipboard and shouted, "Daniel Ace Doe!"

I rushed to the front desk.

"Follow me," she said.

She led us to the exam room, and a minute later, a pediatrician entered. He asked a few questions, rubbed his stethoscope on his palm, placed it on Kevin's chest, and moved it around, listening intently. He repeated this process twice, focusing on his examination. After draping the stethoscope around his neck, he turned to me and said, "You need to take him to the emergency room across the street right away. We'll call ahead to let them know you're coming."

I didn't ask questions. I just did as I was told.

In the emergency room, we were met by Doctor Macek, a short, feisty woman around sixty years old with a thick Eastern European accent. She took Kevin from my arms, placed him on an exam table, listened to his lungs, and immediately ordered a chest X-ray. Before I could inquire about my son's condition, we were whisked away to the X-ray room. It was clear that whatever was wrong with Kevin was serious, so I knew it was best to let the doctors do their job and wait to ask questions later. They took Kevin from my arms and positioned him in an X-ray contraption that supported his small body under his arms and then clamped around his neck. From behind the protective window, all I could see was his head, fire-red from screaming.

After the X-ray, I held Kevin in my lap, comforting him as we awaited the results. I called Linda and Danny, informing them that we were now in the hospital emergency room. Doctor Macek returned, slipped the X-rays onto the light board, and signaled for me to come closer.

"How long has he been like this?" she asked, with a stern gaze on me.

"For a few days," I replied. Despite my response, I sensed that she didn't fully believe me. Her skeptical smirk, which she exchanged with the nurses and residents gathered around, confirmed my suspicion.

"No, this is not just a few days," she stated, her tone accusatory. Was she blaming us for neglecting his cold? At that moment, my sister arrived.

"Are you the mother?" a nurse asked.

"No, this is my brother," Linda responded, shaking her head. "I'm the baby's aunt."

"Hmm…" Doctor Macek stroked Kevin's head. "I recognize this baby. How do I know this baby?"

"He was brought here last August after—"

"Is this subway baby?" she interrupted. I nodded with acknowledgment. "I was here that night and will never forget when the police bring him in. I didn't know, alive or dead? I see them carry in this baby and… I remember like it was yesterday."

"My partner found him," I said. We're his foster parents for now, but we plan on adopting him."

"Are you a police officer?" a resident asked. Linda chuckled. Doctor Macek cracked a smile for the first time. She understood that when I referred to "my partner," I meant my boyfriend.

"Well, well, well," she said, "this is something special we have here, no?" Again, I nodded. She turned on the light board, which flickered briefly before illuminating the X-ray. "But this... this is not so special." She pointed to a white spot on the image indicating Kevin's lungs. "You see this? This is not a cold. This is serious. This is pneumonia."

I swallowed hard, but without saliva, the dryness stuck like powder in the back of my throat. For a few seconds, my mind and body seemed to drift away, finding themselves in a pale, numb place where I was suspended in mid-air while simultaneously suffocating on inertia. Linda placed her hand on my arm, snapping me back to reality.

Pneumonia? At six months old? How could this have happened? Then it hit me: Had we caused this? Did we kick up invisible toxic dust during the wall demolition? Had it lingered in the apartment and found its way into Kevin's lungs?

Seeing the color drain from my face, Doctor Macek touched my arm and assured me Kevin would recover. "He's in the right place," she said. "We're going to take good care of this special little boy." But make no mistake, she added, if we had waited one more day, his condition would have turned dire. While she didn't say he could have died, her message was clear: don't wait next time.

"So," she said to Kevin, "it looks like you're going to be our guest here for a few days." She was oddly chipper, as if welcoming a long-lost relative home.

"It's pneumonia," I told Danny, my voice trembling as I said the words aloud. "Get here as soon as you can."

"Leaving now," he said.

In the meantime, Kevin was admitted. In his room, a nurse inserted a needle to connect him to an IV line. Another nurse placed a nebulizer mask over his mouth and nose, swallowing his entire face. The steam hissed. A heart monitor beeped incessantly.

Danny's eyes welled up as soon as he saw our baby with a tube in his arm and a mask over his face. He wiped his eyes and leaned over the crib. There we were, in a situation we had never imagined three months earlier, worrying about our son's mortality. The past disappeared into irrelevance. All that mattered was our future, who was clinging to life in the crib.

For the rest of the afternoon, Linda, Danny, and I watched and listened to Kevin breathe. In and out. In and out. A jolting and hypnotic cadence.

Sometime just before sundown, Linda left.

Danny and I stood over Kevin's crib well into the night. Time passed, or maybe it didn't. When our legs cramped and buckled, we slid the one chair in the room closer to the crib—sat on opposite armrests—and caressed Kevin's arms and legs through the slats. Our eyelids drooped, but we wouldn't allow sleep to overtake us.

"Why don't you go home?" Danny asked. "You've been with him all day, and a break will do you good."

Even though I was barely hanging on, I refused to leave.

"Seriously," Danny said, "one of us has to get some rest." He patted the chair. "Don't worry, we'll alternate nights on this thing."

He was right, of course. One of us had to recharge for at least an hour or two in our bed to function the next day. And that chair would provide little comfort for one, let alone two.

I bent over the crib, kissed Kevin's fingers, and lightly stroked his temple with the back of my hand. My hand looked huge next to his tiny head.

Danny put his arm around my shoulder and squeezed. "He's going to be all right," he said.

"I know he will," I said. Danny handed me my coat. "Call me if anything changes." Before leaving, I hugged him and turned back to look at Kevin. The future was uncertain. We didn't know what tomorrow would bring. Or the day after that. The only thing we knew for sure was that pneumonia had just catapulted Kevin to the top of his grandmother's sick and dying report.

Danny didn't sleep at all that night, and despite going home, neither did I. The following day, I returned around 6 am, and about an hour later, my parents showed up. Mom immediately went to the crib. Dad handed me a grease-stained brown bag containing our breakfast: buttered bagels and muffins.

"You guys go home. Freshen up." Dad said.

"We're good," I said.

"Scram," Mom insisted. "We got this."

Danny and I resisted but eventually agreed. When we got home, we laid down on the futon and then the bed. But Kevin occupied our thoughts. Any kind of restorative rest would come later.

We returned to the hospital that afternoon, ready to spend another night in Kevin's room. However, Mom had taken over and was settled comfortably in the chair.

"Get out of here," she said. "Grandma's staying tonight."

"She's not going anywhere," Dad stated. "You guys would be better off sleeping in your own bed at home. I'll come back tomorrow to get her."

For the next three days, we were never without company. Family, friends, and coworkers came and went, visiting Kevin at all hours, day and night. Linda and my younger brother Matthew took turns staying in the late afternoons and evenings. Chuck stopped by once or twice a day, and our former roommate Joe delivered a message from my softball teammates, the Rookies. They were all rooting for Kevin, our future bat boy. Nicholas checked in while making the rounds for his patients and never showed up empty-handed, bringing soup or snacks from the cafeteria. The overwhelming love so many showed for an infant who had started life alone deeply touched our hearts. We realized then that our family, our community, and our village would always be there for Kevin. He would never be lacking love in his life.

With the power of that love, Kevin's condition improved more each day, faster than expected. Doctor Macek delivered good news the morning after the third night: Kevin would be discharged later that day. Although there was still a crackle in his breath, the doctor felt confident enough to send us home with a portable nebulizer. We left the hospital that afternoon.

While Kevin had shown no issue with the nebulizer mask at the hospital, the portable one was a different story. When he heard the motor turn on, he began protesting, kicking his arms and legs. And when the mask was about to cover his face, he screamed at the top (and bottom) of his lungs. Danny and I welcomed the screaming. It meant his lungs were getting stronger. Seeing the medicated steam being suctioned out of the mask and into his airways comforted us. Kevin was back to his old self within a few days and no longer needed the nebulizer.

We returned to work the following week, and Kevin went back to Dottie's. Things returned to normal, but that only lasted ten days until another virus struck.

It all started on a Sunday afternoon when my brother, Matthew, offered to watch Kevin one-on-one for the first time. Danny and I jumped at the chance to see a movie, something we hadn't done since becoming parents.

My brother, a graphic artist and a passionate comic book collector, was a huge fan of movies and television. He could watch the same movie or show over and over again, often knowing every word by heart. His favorites included *Moonstruck*, *Steel Magnolias*, *All in the Family*, and the original *Star Wars* trilogy. We fully expected him to have Kevin speaking, or at least grunting, like Yoda by the time we got home.

But Matt never got the chance.

He bounced Kevin on his lap when he felt something warm and wet. Initially thinking nothing of it, he changed Kevin's diaper, wiped his bottom, put on a fresh one, and continued playing with him. But then, Kevin let loose again, even worse than the first time. Matt lifted him up and away from his lap. Thinking this was part of their play, Kevin giggled and laughed, thoroughly enjoying being lifted high, even if he wasn't dry. Unfortunately, every leg wiggle allowed a mess to escape from his diaper and splatter onto Matt.

When Danny and I arrived home, we immediately noticed a foul odor.

"Watch your step," Matthew warned, rushing in from the bedroom, looking haggard. "It's everywhere. Your son's been pooping nonstop for the past twenty minutes. I think he's possessed."

Danny headed straight for the bedroom and carried Kevin to the bathroom. He placed him in the baby bath chair, rolled up his sleeves, and prepared to clean him up.

Meanwhile, Matt changed into a borrowed pair of sweatpants, stuffed his soiled jeans into a plastic bag, and fled.

Kevin's diarrhea continued relentlessly, even in and out of the bathtub. We went through more than a dozen diapers in just one hour. His once soft brown skin turned coarse, ashy white and lost its elasticity.

"Leave a message with Gail," I said. "We're going to the emergency room right now."

Once again, Doctor Macek was on duty and recognized us right away. We briefed her on Kevin's condition, and she promptly started him on fluids.

"Babies dehydrate faster than adults," Doctor Macek explained. She added that we were lucky we hadn't waited until morning, as his system could have shut down from the sudden loss of fluids overnight. She informed us that the likely culprit was rotavirus, which was circulating in daycare settings and affecting many children.

"Do you know what I think is really happening here?" she asked, smiling.

"What?" I asked.

"I think he missed me," she replied, patting Kevin's head. The subway baby had visited her twice in ten days and three times in the past seven months. And despite the circumstances, she enjoyed seeing him.

With round-the-clock intravenous fluids, Kevin rehydrated and recovered faster than he had from pneumonia. He spent only two nights. And remarkably, the back-to-back illnesses did not hinder Kevin's growth. A tape measure around his head indicated he remained above the 95th percentile. In the end, Kevin survived and emerged stronger than ever.

Kevin's illnesses were the most worrisome experiences of our lives. Looking back, it was during that challenging time when Danny and I truly grew up, turned into full-fledged adults, and became men.

We anxiously awaited the day we'd officially become a family.

FIRSTS

In early April 2001, Kevin learned to crawl, but only in reverse. He'd push up with his arms and slide around the apartment feet first, polishing the floors with his belly like a mop. It took about a week for him to figure out how to coordinate his arms and legs to move forward. Once he did, he became unstoppable. With a baby on the move, Danny and I scrambled to baby-proof our home, turning it into a cushioned, padded, foamed, rubberized, plugged, gated, blocked-off, covered, and bolted-down fortress.

Also in April, Danny and I graduated from the ten-week MAPP (Model Approach to Partnership in Parenting) training classes that had started in February. Well, nine for us since we missed one class due to Kevin's illnesses. Unlike the other aspiring parents in the class, we already fostered a child.

Some people in the class only wanted to foster a child, while others wanted to adopt. Most, if not all, hoped to receive a healthy infant. That's exactly what we had, which made us wonder why Kevin hadn't been placed with a pre-approved foster-to-adopt family right from the start. Did the agency make a mistake by placing him with the Garcias? If Kevin had been placed in a stable, pre-adoptive foster home, the judge would have left him there. However, because he was placed in a home that the judge and ACS had concerns about, it created a lucky opportunity for us to become his parents.

The classes were held in a plain conference room at Talbot Perkins. Tables were arranged in a U-shape with an easel holding a giant pad at the top of the U. We always sat in the middle of the U against the wall near the door. During one class, the teacher asked everyone to call out different forms of discipline and then wrote them on the pad. The list included "time outs" and "grounding." Someone in the back shouted, "Spanking," causing a gasp from others.

Nevertheless, the teacher added "spanking" to the list. When the ideas ran out, the teacher took a marker, drew a thick, dark line through "spanking," and said firmly, "We do not hit foster kids. Never, ever." Although both Danny and I were spanked as children, we wholeheartedly agreed that striking a child was ineffective and counterproductive—a needless act of violence.

Around the same time our MAPP training ended, Gail had also completed our interviews. She compiled her notes and finished the home study report by mid-April. Everything progressed as expected, except for the termination of biological parental rights, which remained the only hurdle left on our path to adoption.

Before biological parental rights could be terminated, an effort had to be made to find the parents. This was done by placing public notices in newspapers. We prayed the notice about Kevin would be printed in a tiny font and buried in the back. Our future as a family was at the mercy of timing and literacy.

Danny and I kept a low profile until we were certain Kevin would officially become our son. We avoided discussing how we became his parents so we could continue being his parents. However, we couldn't prevent friends and friends-of-friends from retelling the story. Gradually, the story took on a life of its own, spreading like an urban myth. As the story was retold, people added embellishments and distorted facts, resulting in versions that were far different from the truth. One version that reached us described the baby almost falling onto the subway tracks before grabbing Danny's hand just in time.

Occasionally, through the grapevine, the story found its way to a reporter or television producer. One such producer had heard it from a waiter at Cowgirl, a restaurant we frequented. He represented a well-known celebrity who had an idea for a news magazine show that focused on heartwarming stories, and they wanted to feature our story in a pitch to ABC. While we loved the idea of showcasing positive stories on television, we were hesitant to go public and potentially jeopardize our adoption. Besides, neither of us wanted to wake up with a camera and boom mic in our faces, so we declined.

One evening in late April, as Danny, Kevin, and I sat down for dinner, the phone rang. I looked at the caller ID and saw that it was Gail. Our conversations with her always began with questions about Kevin's well-being.

"He's eating at the moment," I replied. "There's mush all over his face."

"He's a bit messy," Danny chimed in.

"Good to hear," Gail said. "Sorry to interrupt dinner, but I need to know if you guys have a lawyer."

"A lawyer?" I questioned, momentarily panicked. We would only need a lawyer if someone were contesting Kevin's adoption.

Danny paused and leaned in to listen closely. "Why do we need a lawyer?"

"For the adoption," Gail responded matter-of-factly, assuming we already knew it was necessary.

"Oh," I said with relief.

This was the first time we had heard about needing a lawyer. We had assumed that on the day of the adoption, we would go to court, the judge would grant the adoption, and we would leave as Kevin's legal parents. After all, that had been the process for becoming his foster parents, and we hadn't needed a lawyer then. However, upon reflection, it made sense. The ACS attorney represented the state, while the Legal Aid attorney represented Kevin. No one was there to represent us.

"The court could appoint one for you," Gail informed us. "If you need one, let me know as soon as possible."

Fortunately, we had my sister, whom Danny had affectionately nicknamed "Our Lady of Good Counsel" or "OLGC" for short. Linda was admitted to the bar in both New Jersey and New York, so she was capable of representing us in Manhattan Family Court. We just needed to ask.

The following weekend, we paid her a visit. As soon as we parked in Linda's driveway, she opened the back door and snatched Kevin with a cheerful "Hey, little man," carrying him inside.

"We have some exciting news for you," Danny said.

"You're going to be our adoption lawyer," I finished his sentence assertively, leaving no room for her to refuse. She took a moment to process this.

"Good one," she replied, bouncing and rocking Kevin. "I teach tax law. I don't know one iota about adoptions."

"You weren't a politician until you ran for office," I argued. "But you're a fast learner. How hard could it be?"

Linda paced back and forth and took a deep breath.

"I'll ask a colleague," she pivoted.

"We don't want a stranger," I countered. "You can handle it."

"I know I can handle it. The question is, can I handle it well?"

From a legal perspective, she worried about missing important details that an experienced adoption attorney would naturally catch. But while Linda didn't want to make mistakes, the precious boy in her arms needed her. So I used him as leverage.

"How cool would it be if your Aunt Linda represented your Papa and Daddy for your adoption?" I gently rubbed Kevin's cheek as it hung over my sister's shoulder. "What's that? You think it would be totally awesome. You are one smart baby. 'Oh, please, please, Aunt Linda, do it for me. I'll be your best nephew, I promise.'"

To further twist her arm, I reminded Linda of all the work Danny and I had done for the campaign. The website, the banners, the events, the phone calls, the late-night poster hanging, and most importantly, rescuing her car from repossession (a story for another time). This tactic proved effective, and Linda agreed to brush up on family law, specifically regarding adoptions in New York State.

By the end of April, spring had finally sprung. After enduring a long, cold winter, it was such a relief for us to spend more time outdoors. We began exploring the neighborhood playgrounds, the same ones we used to pass by without giving them a second thought. Kevin's favorite was the playground located at the intersection of Bleecker, Bank, and Hudson Streets—it had a sand pit. We liked it because it was safe, clean, and situated in the West Village, where we hoped to meet other gay dads. Unfortunately, we didn't come across any. We knew they existed somewhere as recent newspaper and magazine articles documented the beginning of the "gayby boom," of which we were a part. However, at the time, it seemed like we were the only ones publicly showing it.

Whenever Kevin and I went to what we called the Bleecker Street playground, we always found ourselves surrounded by other kids accompanied by their nannies. Most of the nannies seemed to be of Caribbean descent. On one occasion, a nanny who was sitting next to us asked about my wife's ethnicity, wondering if she was black or Latino. I was tempted to respond with a clever remark like, "He's neither," but I doubted she would appreciate or understand the humor. This kind of scenario happened a few more times with other nannies, and each time, I chose to say that my son was adopted rather than going into a long explanation about our family situation.

During that same spring, the Rookies kicked off our fifth season, and Danny and I took Kevin to opening day. When we arrived at the fields, I helped Danny set up a blanket on the lumpy brown grass behind our dugout. Then, I laced my cleats, stretched, and tossed the ball with Joe to warm up. Meanwhile, Danny placed Kevin, sporting a red Rookies T-shirt and a floppy fisherman's hat, in the center of the blanket. Kevin sat upright, his eyes wide open, taking in all the sights and sounds around him.

Naturally, with a new little fan on the sidelines, pre-game batting practice came to a halt. My teammates gathered around the blanket, eager to see our new recruit. Those who hadn't attended the baby shower were meeting the "mythical" subway baby for the first time. Joe placed a softball in Kevin's hands. It rolled off his tiny hands. Undeterred, Joe cupped Kevin's hands and put the ball inside. Kevin bounced and squealed with excitement, but the ball slipped out again. He looked at Joe, then at the ball, then back at Joe as if to ask, "Aren't you going to get it and give it back to me?" And so, Joe did just that. Even though the softball was too big and heavy for Kevin to grip or control, he loved playing this game of fetch with Joe. They continued back and forth a few more times before Joe left the ball by Kevin's side and returned to practice. Symbolically, you could say Kevin threw out the first pitch of our 2001 season, which meant the Rookies were off to a promising start.

Kevin at a Rookies game

Throughout that spring and summer, we brought Kevin to almost every game. As the season progressed, something incredible happened—the Rookies started winning games. For the first time since we started as a team five years earlier, we ended the regular season with more wins than losses. And the miracles continued in the playoffs. We staged late-inning comebacks, pulled off improbable upsets against dominant teams, and ultimately claimed the championship. It was inexplicable how we suddenly became so skilled. Very little had changed from our previous losing seasons except for one addition—we had a good luck charm cheering us on.

Most weekends, after the games, the three of us would head to my parents' house. Danny and I would make a beeline for Shop Rite, a spacious and affordable supermarket unlike those in the city. We'd stock up on baby food, diapers, wipes, and other groceries needed for the upcoming week. And, of course, my parents would always insist on slipping their credit card into my or Danny's hand. "Take the card and use it," they'd insist.

    Although he was their third grandchild, Kevin was the first to live nearby as an infant and toddler. My brother Joe's two boys lived in Singapore and Sydney during their early childhood. Mom once told us about a neighbor who said, "They're adorable, but there's nothing like having one of your own," referring to Mom's three adopted grandchildren. Mom let remarks like that roll off her back. She had learned to ignore ignorant comments after my brother Matt and I came out as gay. As far as my parents were concerned, dumb people said dumb things, and all three of their grandkids were their own.

    I always felt guilty using their credit card to pay for our groceries. Growing up, my parents often struggled to pay the monthly bills. Because we lived in a conservative upper-middle-class town in one of the wealthiest counties in the country, I didn't fully realize how tight money was at times. But as I got older, I noticed how my friends received whatever they asked for and a weekly allowance. We didn't get an allowance. Instead, my siblings and I got jobs. We started paper routes the second we turned twelve. For a few months, I had two routes. Some of my parents' so-called friends criticized and mocked them for being cheap. The remarks, often made to their face and in front of us, their children, hurt my parents deeply. But Dad deflected with humor and joked, saying, "I'm not cheap, I'm economical."

    My parents' financial situation is much better today, and they spare no expense for their grandkids. They have been exceptionally and excessively generous with Kevin and us. It's their way of making up for lost time, giving him the things they couldn't give me when I was his age. So even when Kevin didn't need six pairs of shoes, a dozen onesies, or three ill-fitting winter coats, I couldn't take the giving spirit away from them. "One stays here," Mom justified her purchases, "the other you take, and the third just in case."

Kevin said his first word at my parents' house in late June 2001. It wasn't "Dada" or "Papa," as we had hoped. We almost didn't realize he had spoken his first word and dismissed it as some random baby sound. Kevin waited in a booster seat at the dining table as my mom tore a bagel into small bite-sized pieces. Danny and I folded laundry on the opposite end. A couple of feet away, my dad leafed through a newspaper on the living room sofa. Kevin watched my dad intently, contorting his body and tilting his head to see past my mom.

"Sam, he's looking at you," Mom said. Dad peeked over the newspaper headlines and started a game of peek-a-boo.

"Hello there," Dad said with a big cheesy smile. But Kevin ignored him.

"Bagel, mummi?" Mom tried to get Kevin to eat. She always added "mummi" to the end of everything she said to him. "Let's get dressed, mummi." "Wash that face, mummi." "What's the matter, mummi?" "Did you go poops, mummi?" It sounded like an endearing ethnic remnant and not necessarily an Italian one.

Kevin pushed her hand away and pointed toward his grandpa.

"Cock," he shouted.

"What's that, mummi?" she asked. Dad rested the newspaper on his lap. Danny and I exchanged confused glances. *Did he just say what we think he said?*

"Cock!" Kevin flexed and jerked his arm, gesturing again towards Grandpa. Was Kevin calling his grandpa "cock?"

"What did you say, Kev-O?" Dad asked. "What did he say, Louise?"

"I can't repeat it," a red-faced Grandma giggled.

"Cock!" Kevin said, determined to be understood. Dad furrowed his brow as if the only place his grandson could've picked up the word was from one of his gay dads. Except he spared Danny and glared at me.

"Don't look at me," I said defensively, "you and Mom have been with him all day."

"What's that you're pointing at, mummi?" Grandma asked.

Danny traced an invisible line from Kevin's finger to the grandfather clock on the wall above the grandfather. At that moment, the clock chimed. BONG! BONG! BONG!

"Do you mean 'clock,' mummi?"

"Cock! Cock!" Affirmative. Kevin bounced with excitement. Finally, we understood what he had been trying to tell us. We clapped and cheered. Our son had spoken his first word: C-(silent L)-O-C-K.

"Da-da" would happen a week or two later.

And "Pa-pa" soon followed.

ONE STEP AHEAD, ONE STEP BACK

    The adoption countdown clock bonged and ticked slowly, making us feel like we were living in limbo. We had a son and were a family, but it wasn't official.
    In late July 2001, Kevin took his first steps. Danny and I had been lifting him to his feet for about a week, but he couldn't find his footing. His legs would buckle, causing him to collapse to the floor. At that point, he was a masterful crawler with little need for this walking thing. But then, one night, we propped him up, and he steadied himself against the coffee table. His eyes grew wide, and he was in awe of himself standing. Excited, he bounced. Then plop, he landed on his bum and bounced again to signal us to lift him again. For the next few days, we repeated this over and over. Eventually, we held up his arms and walked him around the apartment. It took him a week to attempt walking on his own.

It happened one night while I was cooking dinner behind the safety gate in the kitchen. Danny let Kevin go and braced him with one hand from behind. "He's coming to get you, Papa," Danny alerted me as I turned around. Kevin took a shaky step forward, followed by a wobbly step back and did a hula dance before moving forward again. It was quite a balancing act. "Go to Papa," Danny cheered.

I knelt to be at eye level with Kevin and reached my hands over the gate. "Come to Papa, Kevin." His eyes remained wide but focused and determined. "You can do it," I reassured him. Danny continued encouraging him from behind, and I did the same from the front. The distance was pretty close, at most four feet. But it took about five minutes of starts and stops, a couple of plops and resets, until he reached the gate. His final steps came in rapid succession, and when he grabbed the gate, he screamed with delight. I planted a big kiss on his cheek, turned him around, and told him to walk back to Daddy, who waited with open arms by the sofa. Instead, Kevin dropped to the ground and crawled over, his way of saying that he had done enough work for one night. However, he would be up again, stronger and faster, exploring his environment freely and reaching for things he couldn't before, especially the volume dial on the stereo receiver.

That same month, Kevin's biological parent's rights were terminated almost exactly a year from the day he was found. But even though he was now freed for adoption, it didn't mean we could adopt him right away. His status had to be verified by ACS, and all the necessary paperwork needed to be completed with careful attention to detail.

Saturday, September 1, 2001

We celebrated Kevin's first birthday over Labor Day weekend with a barbecue in my parents' backyard. The weather was perfect—clear skies, low humidity, and temperatures in the low seventies with a cool breeze. My mom dressed Kevin in a white sweatsuit, making him look like the Pillsbury Doughboy but with a chubby, brown face. Danny and I set up chairs and snack tables on the lawn while Mom decorated the side of the garage with a "Happy Birthday" banner and tied balloons to the planter hooks under the gutters. Around 1 pm, guests started to arrive. Mom gave everyone a homemade, cone-shaped cap with a crayon-drawn number 1. Dad fired up the grill, and the party began.

Later in the afternoon, after we had eaten all the hot dogs, burgers, chicken, sausage, and salads we could, Mom brought out the birthday cake. Normally, she would bake and decorate the cake herself, but this time, she ordered a special Elmo-themed cake for Kevin. She put Kevin in the seat clamped to the picnic table and called everyone over to sing. Kevin seemed confused but joined in anyway. Then he wasted no time diving into the cake icing. We let him use his hands instead of using a fork to feed him. Soon enough, his face was a sugary red mess.

Kevin's first birthday

He had picked apart and eaten almost a whole slice of cake when an unexpected guest crashed the party. A rabid raccoon, foaming at the mouth, hobbled out of the bushes. Guests screamed and rushed to get inside the house as if Freddy Krueger himself had just appeared and started slashing a chaise lounge.

A neighbor, who had been tracking the raccoon, emerged from behind the hedges with a pitchfork and a large garbage pail. He and my dad worked together to handle the situation. Dad lured the raccoon away from the party so the neighbor could trap it under the pail. Once they captured it, they placed a cinder block on top and backed away, waiting for the police and animal control to arrive.

This was the second time in as many birthdays that calls to 911 had brought first responders. Kevin was batting a thousand. We just hoped the raccoon wasn't an omen for the year ahead.

Tuesday, September 11, 2001

That morning, like every other, we went about our routine—diaper change, breakfast, showers for us, dressing Kevin, and then taking him to Dottie's. I had just come out of the bathroom when Danny pointed to the television. Plumes of black smoke billowed from one of the Twin Towers. Since we were running late, we didn't think much of it, turned off the TV, and rushed out the door. I walked Danny and Kevin to Dottie's, hugged and kissed them, and headed to the office. When I arrived, my cubicle neighbor wasted no time telling me the country was under attack.

I called our cell, hoping to reach Danny before he boarded a downtown train. His office was less than a mile away from the World Trade Center. I couldn't get through, so I called Dottie. Danny and Kevin were still at her place, safe and sound.

Lower Manhattan was off-limits for several weeks after the attacks, and the National Guard erected a checkpoint just outside our apartment building. Unless you lived there, downtown below 14th Street was restricted. We had seen and heard a lot through our windows—fires, accidents, protests—but never the presence of the military. Armed guards blocked off the Village. As the cleanup progressed, the blockade drifted further south. However, the Family Court building, closer to Ground Zero, remained inaccessible.

About a week after 9/11, Danny's folks called to express their desire to visit and meet Kevin. They hoped to arrive in mid-October. Danny scouted nearby hotels and bed and breakfasts, but none fit their budget. That's when my parents stepped in and offered their house in New Jersey. Danny told his parents, and they accepted.

In the days leading up to their visit, I worried about the arrangement and prepared myself for any potential awkwardness, envisioning a Stewart/Mercurio version of *Meet the Fockers*. The idea of my northeast, liberal, Catholic, and gay rights-advocating parents hosting his Bible-belt, conservative, Southern Baptist parents made me anticipate a potentially long and uncomfortable weekend.

Danny and I picked up his folks at the airport and brought them to my parents' house. My dad greeted us in the driveway and quickly broke the ice by welcoming Danny's folks to his "sprawling estate." Mom brought Kevin straight to Danny's mom, saying, "Here's your grandson." Smiles were shared all around as Kevin was passed from one grandma to another.

Over the next few hours, our parents got to know each other. My dad peppered Danny's dad with questions about what it was like living in the country while my mom shared everything Danny's mom wanted to know about Kevin. Surprisingly, despite their different backgrounds, opinions, and world views, the in-laws-to-be got along exceptionally well.

My parents proved to be hospitable hosts, and Danny's folks proved to be gracious guests. They hit it off so well that Danny and I left Kevin in their care one afternoon. They took him to the county zoo, where they rode the miniature train, fed the animals, and snapped a ton of photos. Later that evening, over a plate of steaming pasta, Danny's parents invited my parents to visit Texas. Dad appeared excited about the idea, but unfortunately, he had an aversion to flying, and driving would take too long.

December 14, 2001

ACS verified that Kevin had been freed for adoption. Next, a document titled "Notice of Application for Review of the Status of a Child Freed for Adoption and Petition for Review of the Status of a Child Freed for Adoption" was served on February 7, 2002. We were making progress. A permanency hearing was scheduled for March, and that's when Linda made her first court appearance on our behalf.

As two unmarried men in New York, we were uncertain about whether we would be permitted to adopt Kevin together. Linda explained that the law was murky and confusing. At the time, the law allowed either an adult unmarried person or an adult husband and wife to adopt another person. Individually, we qualified as unmarried adults, but as a couple, we didn't fit the husband or wife requirement. This meant that we would have to adopt Kevin separately. Danny would go first, and then I would adopt Kevin as a second parent or co-parent soon after. We were determined to do whatever was necessary.

However, Linda discovered a potential solution while researching adoption law. She came across a 1995 ruling by the Court of Appeals, New York's highest court, that allowed unmarried couples, regardless of sexual orientation, to adopt. The decision on whether such an adoption would be in the child's best interest was left to the individual judge's discretion. In simpler terms, a family court judge in Syracuse could deny a same-sex couple the right to adopt jointly, while a judge in Manhattan could grant them that right. This meant that a joint adoption for us was possible, or at least not legally impossible. Since we believed Judge Cooper would likely approve our adoption as an unmarried couple, Linda suggested that we petition the court for a joint adoption. We were willing to give it a try.

We were not present in court on the day Judge Cooper received our adoption petition. We heard from Gail and Karen that she didn't flinch when she saw both our names. This was a huge relief. Linda summed up the situation by saying, "The judge allowed it. She did not have to. Even if she supported gay adoptions, she could have required you to adopt Kevin individually via two separate adoptions. No one else had the standing to object. I suppose if someone at the SSA [Social Security Administration] wanted to make a fuss, they could have. That would have meant the birth certificate would not have been issued with both your names. Either no one at the SSA noticed two male names on the certificate request, or they simply didn't care. A lot of pieces just fell into place."

Right from the start, the dedication and support of everyone at Talbot Perkins had been crucial in ensuring the smooth progress of our adoption process. Unfortunately, things were about to change. Without warning, Gail informed us that the agency would be closing down at the end of the month. She assured us that the transition to the new agency, Episcopal Social Services (ESS), would be seamless, and she would stay with us until the end.

Danny and I met our new caseworker at ESS on March 20, 2002. ESS operated efficiently, like a well-oiled machine. We immediately felt secure and knew we were in good hands. Our new caseworker informed us that they would need to conduct their own home study, which meant starting the process all over again. It felt like a step backward.

"What about the parent training classes? Do we have to retake those?" Danny asked. She shook her head, explaining that our credits transferred. Our adoption journey continued smoothly throughout the summer of 2002, and we were relieved when our second home study was completed quickly and without issue.

As autumn arrived, Linda worked on finalizing the Certificate of Adoption. All the necessary paperwork had been completed by late October, with every detail filled in and signatures obtained. There was just one thing left to do: choose a date. Although we were eager to solidify the adoption as soon as possible, we also felt it would be special to have Kevin's adoption take place on December 22nd, the same day he came home two years earlier. Unfortunately, that day fell on a Sunday. Besides, the judge was only available on Tuesday, December 17th. Close enough. We confirmed the date. Soon, our family would be officially official. Just in time for Christmas.

FAMILY

Tuesday, December 17, 2002

After a light breakfast, we dressed Kevin in khakis and a button-down shirt. He looked in the mirror to examine his spiffy threads. He knew this was no ordinary day. In the preceding weeks, Danny and I talked to him about going to court and his adoption, explaining what the day was about.

"But we are a family," he said during one of those conversations, sounding confused.

"That's true," I said. "The judge is just going to make sure we stay a family."

"Forever," Danny added, emphasizing my point.

"Oh," Kevin replied, seemingly satisfied with our response. For all he knew, every family needed a judge to make them permanent. There was no need to over-explain.

Kevin sprinted from the bedroom mirror to the apartment door. "Papa!" He summoned me. "Pick me up." He gripped a foam basketball in his right hand and waited beneath the plastic net. "Papa!"

"Papa's getting dressed," Danny said. "Let's take a few shots without him." Kevin pouted, sat on the mat, and waited. For some reason, he preferred to play ball with me and would rather wait than play with Danny.

I adjusted my tie in the bedroom, catching Danny's reflection in the mirror.

"Papa!" Kevin shouted from the living room.

"He wants you," Danny said. "But we don't have much time."

We rarely dressed up. Danny looked so handsome. He wrapped his arms around my waist and rested his head on my shoulder.

"A few hoops," I said, "and then we'll go."

Kevin jumped up as soon as I entered the living room. I lifted him high in the air so he could slam dunk. We continued doing that a few more times until it was time to leave and trade our make-believe basketball court for a very real family court.

Linda and my parents met us in the waiting area. Kevin, thrilled to see them, ran over and gave each of them a big hug. As my parents, Linda, and Danny engaged in small talk, I stepped away and paced the room.

The enormity of forever suddenly overtook me. *This is it. After today, we'll truly be on our own. Kevin's fate will rest solely in our hands.* Thoughts of the future consumed my mind. What kind of person will Kevin grow up to be? Will he be kind, compassionate, neurotic, inquisitive, impulsive, thoughtful, pompous, introverted, or outgoing? Will he become a writer like his papa, a social worker like his dad, or a lawyer like his aunt? Will he be nagged and troubled by questions about his identity and where he came from? How will he handle all the questions that were sure to come? Will Danny and I have succeeded in raising him to be confident and poised enough to deal with it all? A hand touched the back of my arm.

"They're ready for us," Danny said.

Judge Cooper smiled warmly as we walked in, acknowledging each of us. Her face lit up when she laid eyes on Kevin. It was their first meeting, and the child for whom she had made countless decisions was finally there in person. We sat behind the lawyers' table, with my parents sitting behind us in the back of the courtroom.

I turned around and caught a glimpse of my parents. Mom clutched a tissue. Dad nodded his approval. They were about to become newly minted grandparents. Their family, much smaller and less Italian than they had ever imagined, was about to grow by one. And to them, family meant more than just blood.

Kevin straddled my left leg and Danny's right. He looked back at his grandparents, then surveyed the entire courtroom, observing every detail—from the stenographer adjusting her position to our caseworker opening a folder to the guard standing with folded arms. His eyes darted up, down, and all around until they finally met Judge Cooper's. She waved, and Kevin waved back. A smile, two years in the making, bloomed on her face.

Linda stood up to address the court.

Kevin waved his arms, motioning for her to sit down, not understanding why his Aunt Ni-Ni (as he called her) stood while the rest of us remained seated.

"Ni-Ni," he called out, "Sit down!"

"It's okay, Kevin," Linda turned around to explain. "Aunt Ni-Ni is allowed to stand. I'm representing your Papa and Daddy."

"Who do we have with us today?" Judge Cooper asked, referring to my parents in the back.

"These are the baby's grandparents, your honor," Linda replied.

"Welcome," the judge said warmly. "I'm so glad you could be here. This is a very special occasion."

"Yes, it is," Mom said. Dad nodded in agreement.

"Shall we begin?"

Linda presented the Certificate of Adoption without delay. Judge Cooper quickly scanned the document, held it up, and grinned.

"You guys ready?" the judge asked. We nodded and stood, with Kevin supported on the table by us from behind. Now at eye level, the three of us were seconds away from officially becoming one family unit.

9:45am

Judge Cooper flipped to the signature page, lifted her pen, glanced at us one last time, smiled, and signed her name. In a single stroke, Daniel Ace Doe became Kevin Stewart-Mercurio, and we became a family forever.

"Congratulations, young man," Judge Cooper said to Kevin. "And to you too, gentlemen."

Everyone applauded, including Kevin. He wrapped his arms around our necks and squeezed tightly for a double-clutched family hug. When he let go, Danny and I let out an audible sigh of relief. The breath we had held for two years escaped. It was official. We could finally relax.

Judge Cooper politely tapped her gavel, indicating that our celebration needed to continue elsewhere. We couldn't linger. But in the two years since Kevin had become our foster child, one question remained unanswered.

A big one.

The one that had changed our lives forever.

Why did Judge Cooper ask Danny to adopt? This question often lingered in our minds. Did the idea come to Judge Cooper after she discovered that Danny was a social worker? Or did she spontaneously decide he would make a suitable parent after hearing his testimony?

"Your Honor?" I hesitantly raised my hand.

"Yes?" she asked.

"Um, we..." I stuttered. "Uh, we've been wondering for the past two years why you asked Danny if he was interested in adopting?"

"I had a hunch," she said curtly. "Was I wrong?" She raised an eyebrow and smirked.

Fearful that she might reconsider, we quickly shook our heads.

Satisfied with our answer, she stood up, congratulated us again, exited the courtroom, and departed from our lives forever.

A hunch? That was it? Just a hunch? Her answer only invited more questions, which would also remain unanswered.

As we made our way out, Linda whispered in my ear, "You done good, Lollie." Observing Kevin and Danny holding hands and seeing my parents beaming with pride, I realized Linda was mistaken. We hadn't done good. We got good.

With Kevin's future now resting on our shoulders, Danny and I stepped outside the courtroom and continued to do what we had never dreamed or anticipated we would do, but what the universe had entrusted us to do: provide a stable home for a forsaken infant, our boy, our son, and love him with all our hearts.

Unconditionally.

Every day.

For the rest of our lives.

FOREVER

All of us have the fundamental need to belong and be loved.

Judge Cooper

SKIN DEEP

We received Kevin's birth certificate in the mail a couple of weeks after his adoption. Both of our names were listed as parents. It was now more than real. And different. We became fully immersed in our toddler's world and lost touch with much adult life, especially pop culture. It finally made sense why my parents would say they missed out on so much music, movies, and television from the 1960s and 1970s because they were "too busy raising kids."

As parents, Danny and I found that we related more with other parents than with most of our friends. Instead of keeping up with the latest movie releases or television shows, our days were filled with games of hide and seek, countless scavenger hunts, tossing balls, pushing swings, chasing, tickling, wrestling, and roughhousing. We delighted in cuddling, reading books, and snuggling with our boy. We made new friends: Old MacDonald, The Farmer in the Dell, Big Bird, Elmo, The Wiggles, Jay Jay the Jet Plane, Thomas the Tank Engine, Bob the Builder, Blues Clues, and Dora the Explorer.

Whenever we met someone new, the first or second question was, "How did you guys get your son?" Our answers varied in length, sometimes turning into long and detailed explanations. We would indulge in every detail in the first couple of years, captivating the listener. Some people seemed skeptical, while others were simply in disbelief. However, as time passed and we shared our story more frequently, it became more concise. Our shortened version went something like this: Danny found an abandoned baby at a New York City subway station. We went on with our lives. Three months later, a family court judge asked us to adopt the baby. And we did.

Regardless of the length of our response, emotions always got the best of us. While retelling our story, we would inevitably choke up as if we couldn't believe it ourselves. The initial images of that fateful night would play in our minds, and Danny would vividly remember discovering and seeing Kevin for the first time, while I would recall how he yawned in the policeman's arms. That's all it took—those simple memories—and we'd pause to catch our breath and brush away the tears. It was as if we were being transported back in time, reliving the incredible journey. Some days, I still can't fully grasp the reality of it all.

We loved hearing our story retold through someone else's perspective, wondering which details they would emphasize or leave out. Our friend Joe was an exceptional storyteller, narrating our tale with such enthusiasm and passion as if he were reading a fairy tale to a room full of eager children.

Now that Kevin was officially ours, we no longer had to take him to the adoption agency or clinic for medical care. However, we still needed to find a pediatrician for his ongoing healthcare needs. We searched for nearby providers within our health insurance plan and eventually chose St. Vincent's Pediatrics.

As we sat in the exam room, waiting for our appointment, we heard a distinctive accent coming from the hallway. It had been a couple of years since Kevin's hospitalizations, and it never crossed our minds that Doctor Macek might be a part of this practice.

"Well, what do we have here?" Doctor Macek opened the door and looked down at a mostly empty folder. When she looked up and saw Kevin, she was speechless. She glanced at us, then back at him, and grinned.

"My, my, you've gotten so big," she said with youthful exuberance.

The universe sure works in mysterious ways. Who could have predicted that the doctor who first examined Kevin as a foundling and then treated him back to health twice would now be his permanent pediatrician? It was another alignment of luck and chance that had followed us since August 28, 2000. At that moment, we heard the echo of Dr. Macek's words from three years earlier: "This is something special we have here, no?"

In addition to others asking how we got Kevin, they also praised us for being good parents. All the time. The compliments started the day we picked him up, with the nurse calling us naturals. Friends, other parents, teachers, and sometimes strangers told us what a great job we were doing. While we appreciated the praise—it's always lovely to hear—we also found it odd. Danny and I were only doing for our son what any parent would do for their child.

"Ever notice how people tell us how good of a job we're doing with Kevin?" I asked Danny one night as we vegged out on the sofa.

"I know," he said. "What's up with that?"

"Who knows? Have you ever complimented another parent?"

"Never."

"Are we supposed to?"

Danny sighed and patted the sofa, my cue to lie next to him so we could cuddle. Most nights, we unwound in each other's arms until sleep overtook us. It's all we could muster after dinner, dishes, playtime, bath time, pajamas, toy clean-up, book or story time, and finally bedtime, rubbing Kevin's back until he fell asleep.

On the following nights, we talked more about the praise thing. We suspected it had less to do with our parenting skills and more to do with being men—two men, in fact—raising a baby. We floated a couple of theories. Either people found it remarkable that Kevin thrived in the care of two dads, or, more likely, they wanted to support and encourage us.

In addition to praising us, people also made unsolicited comments about Kevin's appearance. They'd say things like, "he's so handsome," "beautiful skin color," or "he's a looker." My mom said some variation of the latter quite often.

"He's going to drive the girls crazy," she said often. A knot formed in my stomach the first time I heard it, but I didn't know why. On the surface, it's an innocuous remark, but still, something about it rubbed me the wrong way. But I let it go.

Then, one weekend at my parent's house, after my parents had taken Kevin to the mall to ride the carousel, I overheard Mom talking to Kevin about a girl at the mall and how she flirted and batted her eyelashes on the merry-go-round. "You're going to be a real heartbreaker," she told Kevin.

Once again, the comment bothered me.

"Mom, he's not a heartbreaker," I said. "He's three. And someday, he may drive girls and boys crazy. I know you're only being playful with him, but, you know, comments like that made it hard for me to accept being gay when I was a kid. I'd feel better if you didn't say things like that."

Mom nodded, understanding. She had witnessed how difficult it was for my brother and me to come out. Besides, at that moment, we both realized it wasn't about whether Kevin turned out to be gay or straight. It was about being sensitive to the fact that he could be either, both, or something else. His self-acceptance was all that mattered to Danny and me. And we would do anything to make his journey towards self-discovery easy and seamless. However, when others commented on his physical appearance, Kevin became very aware of himself.

"Why do people always talk about my skin color?" he asked one morning on a walk to school.

"Well, uh…" I said, pausing to find the right words. "You know how some people lie in the sun to get a tan? Your skin is naturally that color. People wish they had what you have. And you don't even have to lie in the sun to get it." He nodded and didn't ask any more questions.

Out of curiosity, people always asked about Kevin's ethnicity.

"What's his background?"

"Where is he from?"

Others would ask as if they were required to check a box for ethnicity on a survey. When we said we didn't know, they would offer suggestions.

"Oh, oh, oh, I have a friend from Thailand. Your son looks so much like him."

"Ah, he's definitely from South America. Latin American all the way."

"Puerto Rican."

"He could be from India or Pakistan."

"He's Mexican."

"He's definitely a mix. Half-black, half-white, or something else."

"He looks like Tiger Woods. What's Tiger Woods?"

"A golfer," I'd reply with a deadpan smile.

Although it didn't matter to us where Kevin came from, Danny and I had our theories. One night, with Kevin asleep on our laps—his head resting on Daddy and his legs draped over Papa—we discussed the possibilities.

"I think he could be Filipino or Indonesian," I said.

"Nope," Danny said. "He's Samoan or some other Pacific Islander."

"Samoan?" I asked.

"Yes. Think about it. First, he's a giant for his age. Second, he loves being shirtless and barefoot all the time. It's like our apartment is his own little island."

Race and ethnicity don't matter to kids. Kevin knew this: his dad was Texan, and his papa was Italian. So he saw himself as Tex-Italian. And for us, being free from labels was his beauty. He could check all the boxes or none at all. Filipino, Samoan, Mexican, Indian, Swedish? (Okay, he probably isn't Swedish.) Who cares? We didn't. As far as we were concerned, as long as he was comfortable in his skin, he could identify as Tex-Italian for as long as he wanted.

Unfortunately, in the future, he will not always feel at ease with his skin color, particularly in this country. Danny and I will have several conversations with Kevin about the overt and subtle ways he might experience discrimination, mistreatment, or outright hatred. Whether we liked it or not, our son—just for being a person of color, having two dads, or both—will face some form of bias, intolerance, or ignorance. These talks will rattle our souls and break our hearts, but they are ones we must have so he is prepared for a time when we are not around to protect him.

WHERE THERE'S SMOKE

Everyone warns you about the terrible twos. Kevin was an angel at two, but a switch flipped the second he turned three. Our angel became Lucifer. His infectious giggle? Gone. His buoyancy? Sunk. At times—too many to count—he lashed out for no reason. A pint-sized wrecking ball, he attacked his stuffed animals, tore books apart, destroyed his bed, and savaged his toy box. Our home often looked ransacked. It was an inside job, and we knew the burglar.

One frigid evening in early December 2003, I picked up Kevin from the YMCA nursery school three blocks from our home on 17th Street. When we turned the corner onto 7th Ave and were midway to 16th Street, Kevin collapsed to the ground in a rage and started banging his head on the concrete. I crouched down to his level. He screamed, "GO AWAY! DON'T TOUCH ME!" I went to pick him up. "STOP! Put me down!" He kicked and punched. There I was, a white man wrestling a brown boy in front of Pottery Barn.

Kevin had a tantrum almost every day for a year. Like tornadoes, they varied in length and intensity, ranging from an F1 to F5. All of them happened without a discernible trigger. His nursery school teachers said he was an angel, a role model for the other kids. He bottled up all the volatile energy and uncorked it on us, the ones who loved him the most, the ones he loved the most, and the ones he felt safest around to lose all control. Besides Danny and me, only four other people ever witnessed an F5: my parents, Linda, and Chuck.

"I" and "hate" and "you" became Kevin's three favorite words during a tantrum. When words alone didn't sufficiently serve his purpose—if he had a purpose at all—he got creative. One Thursday night, with Chuck over to babysit, Kevin flew into a rage, and the destruction commenced. Stomping, huffing, screaming, sheets yanked off the bed, toys slammed against walls. Danny and I canceled our date night and asked Chuck to go home. As he got ready to leave, an eerie quiet came from the bedroom. Had Kevin calmed himself down? Were his tantrums getting shorter? Kevin strolled into the living room, holding a sheet of red construction paper on which he had drawn a heart.

"How sweet," Chuck said.

"See this heart," Kevin honed in on me. "This is what you did to it, Papa." He ripped the heart in half and let the pieces fall. Then, as calmly as he had come in, he turned around and smugly walked back to the bedroom.

"Wow, that was dramatic," Chuck said.

"This is what he's become," I said.

"He definitely has a future in the theatre."

Nothing could have prepared us for this. Our MAPP training was useless. We read books about challenging and spirited children. We sought help from "mommy" message boards. Timeouts were ineffective. Restraining him by holding him so he wouldn't hurt himself only turned him into The Hulk. We tried calmly staying nearby while he exploded. We ignored the behavior. Our techniques varied, but they all failed. At our wits' end, we knew we needed professional help. We couldn't afford it, but we had no choice. So late one night, hunched over the computer, I compiled a list of child psychologists covered by our health insurance plan. But before we could make any appointments, a miracle happened.

Danny was in the kitchen preparing dinner when Kevin had an epic tantrum in the bedroom. That week, our strategy for managing his outbursts was to ignore them and his behavior. So Danny stayed in the kitchen and continued cooking. Kevin screamed and threw objects against the wall, but Danny didn't budge.

"DADDY! DADDY!" Kevin yelled like a maniac. Danny didn't respond, sticking to the plan. But then he smelled something burning. He went to the bedroom to investigate. Kevin was curled up in the corner, crying and trembling on his bed. Danny entered, and the smell grew stronger. Kevin pointed to the opposite corner, where Elmo was perched on top of a lamp, about to go up in flames.

Danny quickly grabbed Elmo, ran to the bathroom, and threw him into the tub. He turned on the water, creating a red sea speckled with burnt fur flakes.

I arrived home a few minutes later.

"What's that burnt smell?" I asked as soon as I stepped inside.

Before Danny could answer, Kevin came running from the bedroom, screaming, "MONKEY HUG!" He jumped into my arms, clamped his arms around my neck, and cinched his legs around my waist. "Spin!" he demanded. This was how Kevin greeted me every time I came home. Hugs and spins. I raised my arms like a helicopter, ready to take off. "Faster!"

Danny rolled his eyes. "We had an incident," he said.

"Another one?" I asked. I wasn't sure what kind of incident happened this time. In addition to the tantrums, Kevin had recently choked on a grape. Danny had to perform the Heimlich maneuver. Another time, Kevin had shoved a googly-eye up his nose and couldn't get it out. It took an hour with tweezers to extricate the nosy googly eye. "So what happened now?"

"Oh, just more of the same," Danny said, gesturing to the wreckage, scattered train tracks, and a dismembered caboose on the floor.

"What's that smell?" I asked.

"Elmo."

"Elmo?"

"Dinner's almost ready. Kevin will tell you."

During dinner, Kevin sheepishly explained how Elmo had ended up on the lamp. "I was mad," he said.

"Why were you mad?" I asked.

"I don't know."

"What were you mad about?"

"I don't know," Kevin said, with remorse evident in his voice. Sincere remorse, not the fake "I'm only telling you what you want to hear so I can do what I want" voice. I offered my condolences for his burnt buddy, and Danny and I shared knowing grins.

After putting our son to bed that night, I imagined the events from Elmo's perspective. "Ah, Elmo relaxing so nice here on the bed. Uh-oh, Elmo flying. Elmo landing. Elmo feels warm. Elmo hot. Elmo smoking. Elmo burning. Elmo on fire. Elmo too old for this."

Later, we theorized that perhaps Elmo had sacrificed himself for the greater good, self-immolating to bring peace back into our home. All we know is that after the charred muppet incident, Kevin's tantrums stopped. It wasn't the professional help we had sought, but it worked. By then, the year of tyranny had taken its toll. While Elmo's hair got fried, Danny's hair got grayer, and my hair gave up and fell out. We may have aged faster than a two-term war President, but at least we got our sweet boy back.

UNEXPECTED

When out in public as two men with a baby, I was always on the lookout for potential danger from people who looked like they could harm or harass us. It didn't matter where we were—a shopping mall, restaurant, movie theater, or just walking down the street—my antenna was always up. I acted as our family's dedicated secret service agent, constantly surveying our surroundings, observing people's faces, and noting any nonverbal cues: sideways glances, smirks, whispers, or hostile vibes. Danny saw my vigilance as unnecessary paranoia. He was probably right, but I preferred to err on the side of caution. Better to be safe than sorry.

On one occasion, while riding the subway with Kevin asleep in the stroller, a drunk and unkempt woman stumbled onto the train and accidentally bumped into the stroller's handlebars. I stood up and positioned myself between her and Kevin, ready to take action if necessary. She stumbled and collapsed onto the seat next to Danny, repeatedly looking at me, then Danny, then Kevin for two stops.

"Black or white?" she slurred, leaning against Danny and pointing at Kevin. Danny ignored her. "Where's the mother?" she shouted.

"There is no mother," I answered firmly, feeling my body tense up.

"Who's his mother?" she asked again.

"He doesn't have a mother," I said with a firm don't-fuck-with-me tone.

"Where's his parents?"

"We're his parents," Danny calmly responded, trying to defuse the situation and calm me down.

The woman stood up, swaying unsteadily as she made her way closer to the front of the stroller. I assessed the angles and calculated how I would defend Kevin if she tried to touch him. Her lack of balance made her movements unpredictable, but it also made her an easy target to shove away.

She approached me and extended her arm with an open palm, face up. "All that matters is that this baby is loved," she slurred. "He likes you guys. I can tell." She thrust her hand toward me as if saying, "Put 'er there." Cautiously, I shook her hand. At the next stop, she got off the train, turned to look at us, and punched the air as the doors closed—a drunken salute to our family.

That encounter on the subway was the most direct incident we had ever experienced. Other incidents were more subtle—some involved preconceptions and misperceptions of us as gay dads. But most were internally manufactured dramas created by my inner demons preying on my insecurities.

While Danny and I weren't exactly trailblazers, the big gayby boom was still a few years away. We knew other gay dads existed, but we didn't know any personally. When we did meet other gay dads, we found that we had little in common with them beyond being gay and being fathers. To be blunt, we were in a different socioeconomic class from the gay dads we met. We lived paycheck to paycheck, carried credit card and student loan debts, and had no savings. We couldn't relate to the struggles of finding a reliable contractor to renovate a spacious loft. Instead, we were busy finding the best steel wool to plug holes in our apartment to keep mice out. We were just one layoff, accident, or illness away from bankruptcy and having to live with my parents in New Jersey. Not ideal, but lucky for us, we had some kind of safety net.

In New York City, there is an assumption that gay dads are wealthy. People made that assumption about us. Of course, not all gay dads are rich; it just seemed that way with the ones we encountered. Because we lived in an upscale neighborhood, most parents we met, regardless of their sexual orientation, seemed to have plenty of disposable income. After one of Kevin's first playdates, he came home in awe, going on and on about how his friend had an elevator in their home, not just in the building, but one that opened directly into their apartment.

These differences in wealth triggered my insecurities about providing for our son. I could spend days ruminating over all the things we couldn't give Kevin: a large bedroom with a desk and a PlayStation or Xbox hooked up to a plasma TV, multiple vacations a year, a sibling, or even a pet.

Deep down, I knew that providing material possessions wasn't the only measure of successful parenting. But I couldn't help but question whether we had made the right decision in adopting Kevin. Would he have been better off with the better off? If he had been placed with a wealthy family, he could have had a life of luxury. Danny would remind me that money and material things weren't necessary because we were rich in love. But those thoughts only intensified my inner doubts and insecurities, as they emphasized the fact that love alone couldn't provide our son with his own bedroom.

I often felt inferior, and those feelings led me to become resentful and judgmental. I started viewing all wealthy parents, especially gay ones, as snobby elitists who had it easy while we struggled. And yet, ironically, I also convinced myself that we were somehow better than them because we had to manage some financial hardships.

"We are who we are," Danny would say. "They are who they are. No one is a better parent than the other."

Honestly, I was envious. I wished we didn't have money concerns. I wished we had a sporty SUV parked in a garage, ready to use at will or just on weekends to drive to our beach cottage or country cabin. I wished we could take a nanny on vacation with us. Well, actually, no, I didn't want that. Who goes on a family vacation but doesn't want to spend time with their child?

Then it happened. Another dad let his elitist snobbery slip out. We first met Gary and Zach during an event at the New York City LGBT Center. They lived near us and had two children—an older girl, Olivia, and Jeffery, a boy around Kevin's age. We talked about getting the kids together for a playdate but never made concrete plans. One late spring morning, Danny and I bumped into Gary on the sidewalk after dropping off Kevin at pre-K. After exchanging pleasantries, the rest of the conversation went something like this:

Danny: Your son's also going into kindergarten in September, right?

Gary: Yes. And your son?

Me: Yes. What school will Jeffery be going to?

Gary: City and Country. What about Kevin?

Danny: PS 41.

Gary (disdainfully): Oh. I see you're on a different track.

There it was. Snobbery on full display. Kevin was on a different track because Jeffery's dads could afford $40,000 a year per child for private elementary schools. This one conversation validated all my judgmental demons.

Yes, Danny and I had debt, but we also had reliable jobs and could put aside a little money here and there. We opened a 529 college savings account before Kevin turned one. We saved for an annual family vacation, an option unavailable for truly impoverished families. To them, we probably looked like the elitist snobs. Over the years, I've learned to stop comparing. There will always be people who are better or worse off. The grass is not always greener on the other side. All I needed to do was tend our lawn (if we had one) and stop concerning myself with our neighbors' landscapers.

When Kevin was in second grade, another incident caught us completely by surprise. Harriet, a guidance counselor at Kevin's elementary school, called. Something had happened during recess earlier in the day that left Kevin sobbing. She provided few details over the phone.

I dropped everything and ran to the school. On my way, I called Danny and told him to meet me there. When I arrived, Harriet and Amy, the other guidance counselor—fresh-faced twenty-somethings—showed me to their office, a small, cramped room in the back of the gymnasium. Kevin wasn't there. He had calmed down enough to rejoin his class.

"What happened?" I asked.

"It seems Kevin got very upset when another kid said, 'That's so gay' during recess."

"How did it come up?" I asked.

"Apparently," Amy said, "a group of girls and boys were competing to outdo each other in a game of who could be more gross. One of the girls spit on her hand and held it out for everyone to smell. Then one of the boys put his hand down his pants and did the same thing. And that's when a second boy shouted, 'That's so gay.'"

"We became aware," Harriet said, "when one of the girls told her teacher."

"Was it Kevin who put his hands down his pants?" I asked.

"No, no, but the girl said he was with the group."

Amy explained that they had spoken with each of the kids involved individually throughout the afternoon to better understand the situation.

"And I'm here because…?" I paused, waiting for an answer.

Harriet shifted in her seat. "Have you and your partner talked to Kevin about your lifestyle choice?" she asked.

Lifestyle? Choice? I couldn't believe guidance counselors in a school in New York City's Greenwich Village were using these terms.

"What do you mean by lifestyle and choice?" I asked. "Because we don't see it as a lifestyle or a choice."

"Does he know you're gay?" Harriet asked.

"Of course, he knows," I said, "He's our son." I gripped the armrest, feeling my veins pulse against the plastic. "Was Kevin the one who said, 'That's so gay'?"

"No, but he did get visibly upset when we asked him about it."

"Crying uncontrollably," Amy added. "He had an emotional breakdown. Inconsolable."

I put the pieces together at that moment and understood why I was there: Kevin was upset by their inquiry, not the actual incident. The guidance counselors, in their fact-finding mission, had asked him about the gay comment, which in turn made him feel like they were questioning him about having two dads. It must have made him feel like something was wrong with his family. And being called to their office probably made him think he was in trouble for having two dads.

"Let's wait for my partner, Kevin's other dad, before we continue," I said. Danny could communicate with them on a social worker-to-social worker level. In the awkward silence before he arrived, I tried to calm down.

Finally, ten minutes later, Danny arrived. He listened attentively as they brought him up to speed, thanked them for the information, and calmly said, "We'll talk with Kevin about what happened. It sounds like this might be the first time something like this has happened here at the school. You know, language is important. The words we use are important. I'd be willing to offer a training session for the faculty, administration, students, and counselors." Without raising his voice, he made it clear that they had mishandled the situation.

"That's a good idea," Amy said. "Please let the principal know."

"We will," he said.

As we were leaving, Harriet mentioned that being a parent can be difficult sometimes. It was an attempt to empathize, but to my ears, it sounded condescending.

"Do you have kids?" I asked. She shook her head. "Well, you know, it's not that difficult. Many parents complicate the job and make it harder than it needs to be. Like everyone else, kids need the basics: food, clothing, and shelter. Then they need consistency, stability, security, and love. Everything else is just noise. So being a parent can be easy. Dealing with this kind of stuff is what makes it difficult."

Once Danny and I were outside their office and out of earshot, I let loose a tirade of emotions that eventually ended with "I'm writing a letter!"

"I'll do it," Danny said. He didn't trust me to write something rational.

"To the principal," I said. "And 'cc' the Chancellor and DOE. I'm ready to contact the Mayor, Council Speaker, GLSEN, Family Equality Council, and the media."

"No, no, no," Danny laughed off my tantrum. "We're not doing that. It wasn't intentional. They weren't being malicious.

They're just uninformed. That's all. We have the opportunity to educate them. I'll write to the principal and offer a training." That night, Danny hand-wrote a draft, then left it for me to look at in the morning. I planned to read, edit, and type it up at work the next day. But I forgot to take it with me. The letter sat on the table for a few more days. Then a few weeks. My anger dissipated. The urgency to act passed and the school year ended. We never sent the letter. We decided to revisit the idea of providing a training session at the start of the next school year. We both knew we wouldn't follow through. And we didn't.

We didn't have that kind of lifestyle.

HIS STORY

    Kevin loved listening to stories. From when he was a little child until his preteen years, he insisted on hearing at least one story every night during bath and bedtime. And he wouldn't settle for made-up fairy tales. No, he craved real-life nonfiction: events, surprises, and especially mishaps that happened to his dad or papa. Danny or I would mine our pasts for tale-worthy encounters or incidents. If we repeated a story, Kevin would quickly remind us. "You told me that one already," he'd say. "A new one."
    Most nights, Kevin wouldn't get out of the bathtub until he had heard a brand new story. One of us would sit on the toilet next to the tub, doing our best to entertain. Our reward: Kevin shouting, "Another story!" Bath time would sometimes last for hours, leaving Kevin with skin that looked like a shriveled prune. When Danny took on the storyteller role, he improvised

to create suspense and intrigue. Kevin and Danny would be filled with anticipation, wondering where the story was heading and how Danny would get them there. Since Kevin enjoyed being scared, Danny would often build up to a surprise moment and then jolt him with a quick jerk or a scream. Even a simple, slow-moving story—like Danny driving through Texas—always had a monster jumping out from the roadside bushes.

During our MAPP training, an instructor encouraged parents to create a scrapbook documenting how their foster child became a part of their family. It could be filled with pictures, poems, notes—whatever you wanted. Inspired by this idea, Danny gathered all the necessary supplies—an oversized scrapbook, double-stick tape squares, pinking shears, and markers—and immediately set to work. He collected news clippings, photos, handwritten song lyrics, random words cut from magazines, court summonses, medical reports, and other materials associated with Kevin's adoption.

The empty scrapbook was massive, with numerous pages waiting to be filled. Danny began the project when Kevin was only five months old, and he wanted to fill every page, so he expanded the scope. The scrapbook would document Kevin's origin story and infancy and include milestones and memories from the coming years until the very last page, whenever that might be.

"Could you print out song lyrics for that Creed song?" Danny asked one night. "And the Lee Ann Womack one, too? I want to include them in the scrapbook." Creed's "With Arms Wide Open" and Lee Ann Womack's "I Hope You Dance" came out around Kevin's adoption, and their lyrics resonated with us. The Creed song symbolized our journey to becoming fathers, while the Lee Ann Womack song inspired us to take chances and live life to the fullest. We hoped that as Kevin grew up, he would also take chances and live his life to the fullest. That he'd participate, engage, love, feel, and yes, dance. Danny found a blank page for each song and painstakingly drew the lyrics by hand using colorful pencils.

When he wasn't actively working on the scrapbook, Danny would put it away. In the early days, Kevin would take it off the bookshelf, sit on our laps or between us on the sofa, and flip through every zigzagged cut and glued square. He'd reach a blank page and ask, "When is Daddy gonna be done?"

The final page was adorned in 2011. It took Danny eleven years to shear, draw, and glue his way through Kevin's first three years of life. But it was worth the wait. The final product was precisely everything a scrapbook should be: scrappy, artsy, hodgepodge-y, unpolished, and perfect.

As Kevin grew older, his interest in the scrapbook waned. Now and then, Danny and I would dust off the top edge, sit next to each other on the sofa and flip through the memories. By ourselves, with tissues nearby.

While there were plenty of children's books about adoption, a handful including gay parents, none specifically addressed the way our family was formed. So Danny and I, with help from my brother Matt, created one that did, titled *The Boy from New York City*.

Danny and I wrote the copy. My brother Matt created the graphics by doctoring clip art to fit our story. He photoshopped wrinkles on the clip-art "Danny" and put a baseball cap on the "Pete." He sent me the stylized artwork, and I designed the layout. Once proofread, I printed the spreads on the ad agency's high-res color printers. A coworker in the comp studio compiled, trimmed and spray-glued the pages together. *The Boy from New York City*, without a spine or jacket, may not have been durable, but it served its purpose.

The homemade book opens with two trains, Andy the Express A train and Clara the local C train, pulling into an uptown subway station. In a hurry to get home, Danny runs onto the platform, barely missing the express train. Clara convinces Danny to ride with her instead of waiting for the next express. She tells him the ride would be unforgettable. Along the way, Clara describes to passengers what they could find in the neighborhoods above. Danny exits at 14th Street. Clara reminds him to slow down, saying, "You could miss something special if you move too fast." The rest of the book covers the actual events that happened in real life.

We created *The Boy from New York City* because we wanted Kevin to learn about and feel comfortable with how we became a family. More importantly, we wanted him to hear about his story from us first. Since he was always around other kids, from daycare to elementary school, and most of those kids' parents knew his story, we were concerned that a classmate might overhear their parents talking about how Kevin was found and ask him about it. Any situations where he could learn about his family's story, whether from another kid on the playground, a parent, or our friends or relatives, made us cringe.

Kevin was four years old when we read *The Boy from New York City* to him for the first time. While the book featured our real names and clip-art characters that resembled our family, we didn't explicitly tell him it was about us. We read it like any other book, and it quickly became his favorite, the one he chose to read every night before bed. If he knew the story was about him, he didn't let on. And we didn't drop any clues or hints. We wanted him to connect the dots and make the discovery on his own.

His "aha" moment came about a year later.

One evening, after his bath and getting into his pajamas, Kevin went straight to the bookshelf and pulled out *The Boy from New York City*. It was a typical night, except he seemed more excited and purposeful. He squeezed between us, placed the book on his lap, and tapped the cover—a signal for us to start reading. Kevin knew every word by heart and anticipated when to turn the pages. His page flips were slower this time as if he wanted to savor the story longer. He traced his fingers over the illustrations, connecting with the characters. After Danny and I read the last line together—"They were now all together as a family, making it the best Christmas ever"—Kevin became still and quiet. He focused on the illustration of Danny and Pete holding Baby Kevin in front of the Christmas tree. He reached out and touched the star.

For a few seconds, he didn't say anything. Then he placed his hands down on the book, looked at us, scrunched his face, and asked, "Is this about me?"

"Yes," Danny said, "this is your story."

Kevin furrowed his brows, processing Danny's revelation. Then his eyes grew wide. Huge. We waited for him to react, but he still didn't say anything. After a moment, his mouth opened to a magical smile. He flipped the book over, patted the cover, and shouted, "Read it again!"

Kevin's favorite book

We expected Kevin to have many questions in the following days, but he had none. The story was his, and he didn't need further explanation. He carried the book with him everywhere. Concerned about it getting damaged, he asked me to buy a protective cover similar to the ones for his baseball cards, only bigger. His must-read at night became a must-read in the mornings and afternoons, too. Sometimes we'd catch him flipping through the pages on his own, silently mouthing the words until the end.

Kevin was immensely proud of his family being in a book, and he couldn't wait to share it with his friends. When it was his turn for show-and-tell at school, he knew exactly what he wanted to bring in.

Kevin slipped the book into its protective sleeve the morning of his show-and-tell and carefully placed it in his camouflage backpack alongside his bologna sandwich and baby carrots. On the walk to school, Kevin swung our arms back and forth with more pep than usual. At drop-off, he gave me a quick hug and then dashed inside.

Even though I had no reason to believe he'd get cold feet, I worried about how his classmates might respond. What if their reactions made Kevin never want to share his story again?

Kevin's teacher, Michael, called during lunchtime. While he knew Kevin had two dads, he didn't know how our family came to be.

"Oh my god," he said. "What an amazing story. I had no idea."

"How did he do?" I asked.

"Wonderful, he was great," he said. Then, Michael recounted the morning for me:

> "Kevin, it's your turn," I said. Kevin jumped up to stand in front of the class.
>
> "Are you showing or telling today?"
>
> "Both," Kevin answered.

"So what do you want to show the class?"

"A book," Kevin said. "This book." He held it up.

"What's the book about?" I asked.

"Me," Kevin said proudly, "and my family."

"Shall we read it?"

"Yes!"

"He handled it like a pro," Michael said, "With poise and confidence. Smiling the entire time. We all were."

"So the other kids were okay with…?"

"Yes. Well, some were confused, but I mean, what a story. Here is their buddy, their friend, someone they know, and he's in a book!"

"That's a relief," I said.

"Pete, I don't know what you guys are doing with him, but he didn't flinch. He owned the story. I have to tell you, I got right on the phone with the principal afterward and said, 'You have to hear this.' So I sent him down there to share the story with her."

At dinner that night, Danny asked Kevin how show-and-tell went.

"Great," he said with a brilliant smile.

"I heard you also shared the book with the principal," I said. Kevin looked at me suspiciously—*how do you know that*? "Your teacher called."

"So tell us how it went," Danny said.

Kevin told us all about showing and telling in the classroom and the main office, where the audience included Principal Kelly and Michele, the parent-teacher coordinator. Both listened and flipped through the pages as Kevin told them about his family.

"They really liked the story," Kevin said.

"That's terrific," said Danny.

"Were you nervous?" I asked.

"No, Papa," he answered as if I had just asked the silliest question in the world. It was the first, but not the last, time he would roll his eyes over something I said or did.

Despite how well the day had gone, I still expected some backlash. I feared another parent might resent having to talk to their son or daughter about Kevin's family. Even at an elementary school in one of the most progressive communities in the country, I figured there had to be someone who would get upset about their five-year-old son or daughter's exposure to our family. Sure enough, a week later, another mom had something to say at the next family morning.

Family mornings were monthly events that lasted about forty-five minutes. Parents joined their kids in the classroom to see firsthand what the students were learning. The kids loved family mornings because their parents were there, and it didn't hurt that we brought donuts, muffins, and juice.

That morning's demo lesson was all about math. Kevin dumped a small bag of blocks on the table and began counting. We followed along, adding and subtracting blocks. Then, across the room, I noticed Carly's mom staring at us with laser-like concern. I refocused on Kevin, stacking, making shapes, and counting with the blocks.

Ten minutes later, the teacher rang the bell.

"Family morning is over," he said. "Thank you, parents, for coming. Class, it's time to say goodbye, then return to your tables."

Kevin hugged us goodbye. Danny and I, running late for work, grabbed our coats and left.

Outside, Carly's mom ran up to us from behind.

"Hey, can I talk to you guys?" she asked.

"Sure," Danny said. "What's going on?"

"It's about Kevin," she said.

"What about him?" I asked.

"Well, actually, it's about my daughter. Carly. I, I…want to thank you."

"For what?"

"Kevin really helped her. He was so comfortable with sharing his story the other day, and Carly, well, being adopted herself, she's been struggling with it. His confidence made her feel better about who she is. If he could be so at ease with himself, so could she. So thank you."

"Wow, thanks for telling us," I said.

"Could you thank Kevin, too?"

"We will."

We felt immense pride. That's our boy, being himself and making a difference in someone else's life.

Soon after owning his story, Kevin became more aware of the homeless people in our neighborhood. One morning, while walking to school, he fixated on the ones gathered in front of the church on the corner of 13th Street and 7th Avenue. He kept turning around as we passed, trying to get a glimpse. Then, out of nowhere, he said, "That was me."

"What was you?" I asked.

"That was me. I didn't have a home either until Dad found me."

"Hmm-mmm," I nodded, searching for words. Astonished by his observation, I could only respond, "Well, everyone deserves to have a home. We're lucky we have one."

He observed quietly for the next few mornings, keeping his thoughts and feelings to himself. Whenever I asked if he was okay, he said he was fine. But a few weeks later, on Christmas Eve, he surprised us with an idea.

After caroling in Washington Square Park and visiting Chuck that night, we came home, ordered dinner, and checked NORAD for Santa's location. Danny and Kevin made a batch of chocolate chip cookies. We hummed, whistled, and sang carols while we waited for our food to arrive. We purposely ordered a lot—two pizzas, salad, baked ziti, chicken parm, and meatball parm—so we would have leftovers for the rest of the week.

"In between bites, Kevin asked, 'Do you think they've had dinner?'"

"Who?" I asked, confused about who "they" referred to.

"The people in front of the church," he said, pointing to the leftovers. "Do you think they're hungry?"

"Should we share this with them?" Danny asked.

"Yes," Kevin replied.

"That's a great idea," I said.

After finishing our meal, we combined two half-eaten pizzas into one box, packed the sandwiches, baked ziti and a dozen cookies, and put on our coats. At 10 pm on Christmas Eve, we headed to church.

It was freezing outside, and no one was around. Kevin held Danny's hand while carrying the bag of food. As we approached the church, we saw a collapsed cardboard box on the steps, but no people were in sight.

"Maybe somebody will come back," Kevin said, looking around, hoping to find someone who would appreciate a meal. I suggested that we leave the food on the steps just in case someone did come back. Kevin and Danny agreed. We placed the pizza and package on the top step, in the corner by the cardboard.

"We should leave a note," Kevin said, "so they know it's for them." Luckily, I always carried a pen and notepad, so I retrieved them from my inside coat pocket.

"What should we write?" I asked.

"'This is for you,'" Kevin said.

"And 'Merry Christmas,'" Danny added.

"Yeah, and 'Merry Christmas,'" echoed Kevin. I wrote the note, folded it, and tucked it into the crease of the pizza box. After standing in front of the church for a few more seconds, we turned around and walked home, hand in hand.

Once back, we checked NORAD again. Santa was about an hour away, traveling down from eastern Canada. Kevin hurried to plate some cookies and carrots, a snack for Santa and his reindeer. He placed the goodies on the windowsill and skipped to the bathroom. He quickly brushed his teeth, changed into his pajamas, and went to bed. When we were sure he had fallen asleep, Danny and I wrapped his presents, which we had hidden under our bed, below the kitchen sink, in dresser drawers, and at the back of our two small closets. The year's highlights were a guitar, a beaver hand puppet, and Jose Reyes and David Wright bobbleheads. We arranged the gifts around our tiny tree, poured milk, and ate some cookies, leaving evidence of Santa's visit: crumbs, a bite mark, and a half-eaten carrot.

Even though we never found out if anyone discovered the food we left that Christmas Eve, we learned more about our son and the compassionate young man he was becoming.

CURIOSITY

Most young kids are curious and ask their parents many questions, and Kevin was no different. However, around the time he was 5 to 6 years old, his inquiries went beyond simple curiosity, delving deeper into concerns about his origins, why he was abandoned, and by whom. One weekend, at a playdate, Kevin overheard me telling another parent how he was four months old when he came to live with us.

"Where was I?" he asked that evening at dinner.

"Where were you when?" Danny asked.

"Papa told Ethan's mom I didn't always live here."

"That's true," I confirmed. "You were with a temporary family. They're called foster families."

"And Papa and I were your foster family, too," Danny said, "until the judge made us a forever family."

Kevin listened intently, chewing his food. We could see the wheels turning in his head.

"Do you get it?" I asked. He nodded. "Is there anything else you want to know?" He shook his head. "Well, if you do, you can ask your dad or me anytime."

"We wanted you to be our son," Danny said. "We're so happy we're a family." Kevin reached out for us, pulling us closer, then wrapped his arms around our necks and squeezed. He had a way of strangling us when he was happy.

In the following weeks, his curiosity fluctuated. Questions about his origins usually came one question at a time, not in bunches. He'd ask. We'd answer. He'd mull it over, quiet and reflective, like a detective discovering another clue to solve a mystery. Sometimes, a week or more would pass before he had another question. This cycle of asking isolated questions was (and still is) Kevin's way of gathering information.

He preferred short answers—quick confirmations or denials of his ideas or hypotheses. If Danny or I answered with anything more than a simple yes or no, Kevin would roll his eyes and interrupt us. "You can stop now," he'd say, "I got it." Whenever we started to veer into parental life lesson mode, he'd cut us off with authority: "I don't care. I don't want to know. And I don't want you to tell me."

So we often waited for Kevin to initiate and lead discussions about who he was and where he came from. Many of these conversations occurred during physical activities like walks, trips to the playground, bike rides, or playing catch.

One evening, during a walk to the West Village for dinner at Cowgirl, I asked if he would like to see where he and his dad found each other.

"Yeah!" Kevin's face lit up. "We go after dinner."

"Let's go tomorrow after school when Dad gets home from work."

Danny shot me a look. We hadn't discussed taking him there, and I quickly realized my mistake.

Later that night, after putting Kevin to bed, Danny asked, "You think he's ready?"

"I don't know why I suggested that. Maybe it's a bad idea. But he knows everything. I think he'll be okay."

"All right, let's go," Danny said.

The next evening, the three of us went to the subway exit at 15th Street and 8th Avenue. Kevin walked between us, holding each of our hands the whole way. The dry and cool weather reminded us of the night Kevin was found.

We stood at the top of the steps for a moment. None of us said a word. A trendier and more expensive eatery had replaced the greasy spoon diner that had previously been on the corner. Full-length glass windows replaced the brick wall Danny and I had leaned against. There weren't any smelly garbage bins. The payphones were gone, too. The corner, Kevin's corner, had become more sanitized, the same but different, much like our lives. Danny and I traded glances, cautiously smiling, unsure of how the next few minutes might unfold.

"Ready to go down?" I asked.

"Yes," Kevin replied.

As we descended, Kevin observed everything as if he were seeing it for the first time, perhaps imprinting the images into his memory and linking them to his life story. We turned ninety degrees off the last step and faced the turnstiles. I walked to the nook on the other side, and Kevin followed.

"This is where Dad found you," I said.

Kevin peeked around the bars and stepped into the small, dingy space. Danny and I stood back, giving him room to explore. He studied the ground smeared with grimy, pee-scented subway sludge. He stared at the dark corner, quiet and contemplative. Then, he looked up from the corner and slowly moved his body and head to take it all in like a determined forensics investigator. He examined the cracked paint on the gate and the cruddy, flaky ceiling.

What was he thinking? Had we made a mistake bringing him there? Was he too young? He gave us no clues as to how he was feeling. Danny and I stood by, ready to provide further explanation or comfort.

I worried that we had just traumatized our son by showing him exactly where he was abandoned. Too much, too soon. Why did we do this to him? But that spot was also where our family began. It was a magical and memorable place for Danny and me. Bittersweet. And we wanted him to know about it.

After a moment, Kevin took a deep breath, relaxed his shoulders, and exhaled a long sigh. He turned to us and, without even a trace of melancholy, calmly said, "Okay, we can go now."

That was it. We headed back home.

I wanted to crawl inside his head and make sure he was okay. We had so many questions. How did he feel? What was it like? Did it make him sad? Confused? But we didn't ask. He seemed just fine, and bombarding him with questions could make him think he shouldn't be.

A few days later, sparked by our visit to the station, Kevin wanted to know how babies were born. "Where did I come from?" he asked as we walked home from school. I explained how a baby grows in a woman's belly and that she is considered the baby's biological or birth mom.

"Everyone has a birth mom," I said. "But not all birth moms become parents."

"Who's my birth mom?" he asked. "What's her name?"

"We don't know," I told him the truth.

Danny and I had previously agreed that honesty was the best policy regarding Kevin's questions. We had no secrets to keep, but we also didn't want to create a false narrative.

"Did she leave a note?"

"No, she didn't." The more questions he asked, the more I second-guessed our policy of truth. "But I think she left you where she knew Dad would find you."

My answer seemed to satisfy him.

Even though we didn't know her, Danny and I had mixed feelings about Kevin's birth mom. On one hand, she had unintentionally given us the gift of family, for which we were immensely grateful. On the other hand, she had endangered a newborn's life. Sometimes we felt sorry for her and whatever circumstances drove her to make such a gut-wrenching decision. And yet, we're glad she did.

While Danny and I did our best to answer all of Kevin's questions, we weren't with him twenty-four hours a day, and his schoolmates had plenty of questions for him. It didn't take long until the questioning started to grate on Kevin's nerves. He'd often come home from school at his wits' end.

"They won't leave me alone," he said on more than one occasion.

"Who?"

"The other kids."

"What are they doing?"

"Constantly asking me questions."

"What kind of questions?"

"Who's your mom? Who borned you? It's so annoying. They won't stop, even after I've told them a million times."

Danny and I explained that some of his classmates were probably just confused, and by asking him questions, they were trying to understand so they could be better friends.

"Try not to be mean," Danny said. "You can just say 'I don't know' and walk away."

"But I can't!" Kevin threw his hands in the air. "They follow me around. Everywhere I go. Ugh."

We felt his frustration—deeply. Danny and I wondered if it was too much to expect Kevin to navigate his peers' curiosity on his own. He was still figuring it out for himself. We could talk with him and provide guidance, but we couldn't control his classmates' questions.

We wanted to avoid stepping in, but the situation at school was changing Kevin. He was moody and sour a lot. We had to do something. We needed a firsthand look to get a better sense of the situation. So I volunteered to help with lunch and recess.

As soon as I entered the cafeteria, Spencer, a classmate, rushed over.

"Hey, Kevin's dad," he greeted me, then immediately asked why Kevin didn't have a mom. Kevin rolled his eyes and huffed as if to say, "See, this is what I deal with all day."

"Because he has two dads," I answered politely and smiled. That seemed to satisfy him.

Out on the playground during recess, a girl asked me why Kevin was adopted. "Because his dads love him very much," I said, "and we wanted him to be a part of our family."

"Oh, okay," she said and went back to playing.

I pulled Kevin aside and asked, "Does this happen a lot?"

"Every day. They're making fun of us."

"I know that's how it feels, but I don't think they mean it in that way."

Kevin smirked. It seemed like he understood that his classmates weren't intentionally being mean or annoying. They were just curious. Regardless of the intent, Kevin didn't enjoy the unwanted attention. But there wasn't much he could do about it. By sharing his story, he had inadvertently become a leader. A reluctant leader but a leader nonetheless, both inside and outside the classroom. With our love and support, he would have to find a way to accept and manage the responsibility.

A DREAM

"Do you know who Martin Luther King is?" Kevin asked one night during dinner in early 2009.

"Sure we do," I said.

"It's Black History Month, and we learned about him in school today. Do you know his famous speech?"

"'I Have A Dream,'" Danny chimed in.

"Yes! That one!" Kevin, super psyched that we knew, bounced in his seat. "He gave that speech on my birthday."

Kevin told us more about the lesson at school, and after dinner, I pulled up the speech online. The three of us gathered around the computer. Kevin tapped my shoulder and pointed to the screen.

I have a dream that my four little children will one day live in a nation where they will not be judged by the color of their skin but by the content of their character.

That line struck a chord. We understood that our love and family would have been unthinkable and impossible if we had been born in an earlier era—it would have been just a dream. But thanks to the courage and determination of many equality and justice pioneers, we lived in a time and place where we could be a family. From Martin Luther King to Harvey Milk to marriage rights in Massachusetts, we were the living beneficiaries of the tireless efforts of all the outspoken (and soft-spoken) civil rights activists. We could draw a connection from them to us. We are all connected. One dream on August 28, 1963, led to another dream the same day, thirty-seven years later.

* * *

On the days I picked Kevin up from school, we often stopped at Grounded, Joe, or Jack's, coffee shops along our route that served delicious chocolate chip cookies. Coffee for me and milk for Kevin. While he started on his homework, I tackled the *New York Times* crossword puzzle. We started this tradition in kindergarten. Sometimes, he'd ask for help with his homework, and other times, he'd offer me help for crossword clues. Kevin liked to figure things out, and the puzzle was a tempting distraction from his math problems. He would scan the clues, and if he knew the answer, he would shout out the number, direction, and answer. "22-down is cat!" He would tap the square, demanding I fill it in that second. I worked on the puzzles in ink, so thankfully, he was right more often than not.

One late spring afternoon, when he was in third grade, we got caught in Grounded waiting for a thunderstorm to pass. We stood just inside the door and watched as lightning flashed and rain pounded the parked cars, sidewalk, and window.

"Papa, can I get wet?" Kevin asked.

Playing in the rain was his favorite thing to do, especially stomping in puddles. I looked up at the sky. The lightning seemed to have stopped. It was just raining now. Why not? I thought. We'll dry off at home.

I opened the door and yelled, "Go!"

Kevin darted off and was halfway to the next corner before I caught up. We ran and skipped through the pounding waterfall, splashed in puddles, and dared the clouds for more. I watched my boy kick up water and laugh, a carefree display of joy. I was in awe of him. His being. And in that moment, the world revolved around my son and the rhythmic beating of the rain.

We were drenched head to toe by the time we got home. Kevin slid off his sneakers in the hallway and entered the apartment, shouting, "I betcha you can't get my belly." I took the bait and chased him around the apartment. When I finally caught him, I threw him onto the sofa and tickled and kissed his belly. He laughed and squealed uncontrollably. We were exhausted after a few more escapes and chases around the apartment. Him on the sofa, me on the floor, staring up at the ceiling. Then, out of the blue, Kevin said, "Yesterday is history. Tomorrow is a mystery. Today is a gift. That's why it's called the present."

I was taken aback. Was he reading New Age Zen books?

"Where did you learn that?" I asked.

"Kung Fu Panda," he said.

I should have known. He watched *Kung Fu Panda* every day. Later, as I pulled a dry T-shirt over his head, I couldn't help but think about the present moment—a pure gift.

A dream, actually.

MAKING PROGRESS

We blinked, and time disappeared. Blink! One month gone. Blink! Five years over. Blink! Ten. The rapid pace of time helps explain why infant Kevin didn't blink the first time we held him. He must have known how fast a decade would go and was in no rush to get older.

By the summer of 2010, during the Rookies' fourteenth season, Kevin had become a fixture in the dugout as our bat boy. He fetched hitters' bats and kept them neatly organized against the fence.

As a utility player, I never knew where I'd be on the field or in the lineup. Sometimes I batted second and played second. Sometimes I batted sixth, eighth, or tenth and played first or in the outfield. One weekend in early July, I batted second behind my teammate, Josh, who often led off because he drew walks and ran fast.

Josh and I took practice swings, waiting for the umpire to call "batter up." Kevin stood in the dugout, ready to hand us a different bat if requested.

"Matt talked about you guys on the Assembly floor," Josh said to Kevin and me. "Video's online. Check it out."

"When?" I asked, now pulling on the fence to stretch.

"Last week. On the Assembly floor."

"Really?" Kevin asked.

Josh's partner and future husband, Matt Titone, had recently been elected to the New York State Assembly. In his district, representing Staten Island's North Shore, Matt was the first openly gay candidate outside of Manhattan to get elected to the state legislature. One of our Rookie "wives" had made it to Albany.

"Batter up!" The umpire summoned Josh to the plate.

True to form, Josh drew a walk. Kevin ran from the dugout to grab his bat. "Make sure your dads check out the video when you get home." On his way to first base, Josh called out to me. "It's under 'media' on Matt's Assembly web page."

"Ready, batter?" the umpire asked. I nodded.

As soon as we got home after the game, Danny, Kevin, and I huddled around the computer. I pulled up Matt's Assembly web page and clicked through to the videos. The bill under debate was to permit two unmarried adult partners to adopt a child together.

"I want to be clear to this Chamber," Matt said. "Make absolutely no mistake about it, that this bill…is not about gay rights. It's not about civil unions. It's not about domestic partnership. This bill is about the best interest of a child. Kevin has everything that we think a child should have growing up. He has loving grandparents on both Pete and Danny's sides. He has cousins and aunts and uncles to take him to Disney World and to the Grand Canyon.

"While Kevin may have a whole family, he certainly does not have all the rights of that family. So, I say that this is not about Daniel and Peter, this is about Kevin and his rights and our obligation, responsibility, to ensure that Kevin's rights are fully protected. I will be voting yes on this, Mr. Speaker. I hope today that we all see clearly that this is about children, not about gay rights."

"That was cool," Kevin said.

The adoption bill passed, and the new law removed the ambiguity. Statewide, unmarried couples, straight or gay, could now jointly adopt—exactly what Judge Cooper had let us do eight years earlier. While the bill probably would have passed without Matt sharing our story, we couldn't help feeling that we had played a small role in influencing or changing a vote for progress.

A year later, on June 24, 2011, another critical bill for marriage equality came up for debate in the statehouse. With Matt as a co-sponsor, the Assembly passed the marriage bill on June 15th, sending it to the state Senate for consideration. Danny, Kevin, and I sat on the sofa's edge, watching the Senate vote live on the New York State Legislature's public access channel. Then, at around 10:30 pm, the tally for marriage equality passed the required threshold. All New Yorkers could finally get married.

"YEAH!" Kevin jumped up and pumped his fist. Danny and I embraced. Kevin put his arms around us, turning our embrace into a family hug. A celebration broke out a few blocks south of us as crowds gathered in Sheridan Square next to the Stonewall Inn. We opened the window and looked down Seventh Avenue. Although we couldn't hear any cheering, we did sense the excitement and electricity filling the air that night.

On our walk to school the following day, another dad offered congratulations. Then another parent tapped me on the shoulder and said, "We're so happy for your family."

"It's about time," said another dad.

Even Kevin's friends were ecstatic. "Veronica was so overjoyed that Kevin's dads could finally get married," Kerri, her mom, said outside the school.

All the supportive comments caught me by surprise. Danny and I had never spoken to anyone about getting married. Most of our conversations with other parents centered around our kids, school, playdates, and extracurricular activities.

Even though we were elated by the vote and fully supported marriage equality—we had marched, attended rallies, donated money, signed petitions, written our representatives, and done whatever we could to fight for the right—Danny and I didn't have any plans to marry. My feelings about wedlock hadn't changed much over the years. I was still on the fence about being married. Obtaining the right, for me, was more important than exercising the right. Something about tying the knot still tied my guts in knots.

But now I was curious—how did Kevin feel about all of this? Did he want his dads to get married? A couple of days later, on the second-to-last day of school, I brought it up during yet another walk to school.

"What do you think? Should your dad and I get married?"

"Sure," he said.

"You know, when you were five, we asked you the same question, and you said, 'Ick! No!'"

"I don't remember," he said. "I was five."

"If we were to marry, when should we do it?" I asked. "Our anniversary is July 13th," I continued to think out loud, rambling, "but the law doesn't go into effect until late July, too late for our anniversary. We could do it after. Maybe in the Fall, but I don't want two anniversaries. So what do you think?"

"Sheesh," Kevin rolled his eyes, "just wait until July 13th next year then."

Too cool to be seen with me in front of the school, drop-off now occurred nearly a block away. Kevin leaned in for a half-hearted hug, if you can call him standing just close enough to brush his arm against my chest a hug. He let me put my arm around his shoulder for less than a second before darting off. I watched him run down the block, his backpack swinging from side to side, until he disappeared into the school. As much as I longed for him to give me one last wave goodbye, Kevin never turned around to look back.

    Many people say parenthood is challenging. It is, and it isn't. Early on, you think the hard part is the endless day-to-day tasks and responsibilities. I did. But it's not. That part is easy. It's the letting go that's hard. Drip by drip, your child gets older, and then one day, a vast chunk of innocence breaks off the glacier of his youth forever.

    You experience a million firsts with your child, but there are also a million lasts. The last time he jumps into your arms for a hug, crawls into your bed to snuggle under the covers, asks you to read him a story, dares you to get his belly, plays catch with you for hours, or wants you to walk him all the way to the school entrance. Your child's childhood is fleeting. With every second, the present slips into the past. One day, you're the center of his world, and the next, you're releasing his hand and watching him run down the block alone so he can get his first taste of independence. This is how it should be. To every beginning, there's an end. A first becomes a last. And so, throughout this beautiful journey of raising a child, it's the million goodbyes, the inevitable emptiness, and the wistful longing that are, by far, the hardest part.

    As his elementary school drew to a close, even Kevin could sense the impending transition into a less carefree life. He wouldn't be a young kid for much longer. And sooner than Danny and I would have preferred, he would become a teenager and, before we knew it, head off to college. There were so many times when I wished we could go back to the moment Danny found him and start all over again. Every worry, every diaper change, every scrape and bruise—I would gladly do it all again. If I could go back to those first winter days in 2001 that felt interminable, I'd do it in a heartbeat, lock the door, and savor every single second.

I stood on the sidewalk for a few minutes, keeping my eyes fixed on the space in front of the school where he had just been seconds earlier. I couldn't help but think about my son. That little boy we sang lullabies to every night, and Danny sang "Good Morning to You" to every morning in the tune of "Happy Birthday" had grown up way too fast. Many mornings that spring, I found myself standing on 11th Street, lost in reminiscence. Kevin's early childhood was coming to an end, and soon, we would be saying goodbye to the most unexpectedly wonderful years of our lives. What an honor and a privilege for Danny and me to be his parents and to share in his journey.

Coinciding with the opportunity to marry in the summer of 2011, we also had the chance to move into a new apartment—an affordable, real two-bedroom in a brand new building still under construction in a much quieter neighborhood. The timing was perfect. Kevin may not have realized it yet, but he would soon crave and require more privacy. And with a separate bedroom, Danny and I would no longer have to eat and sleep in the living room. Most importantly, when insomnia struck, I wouldn't have to sit on the bathroom floor in the middle of the night to read.

Besides my parents' house, The Vermin was the only other place I considered home. When I sublet the bedroom in 1994, I never intended to stay for eighteen years. Nor did I ever expect to start a family there. But somehow, that temporary arrangement turned into the only place our son had ever called home. Despite all the angst living there had caused over the years, my heart was heavy. After all, The Vermin was Danny's destination the night he found our son. It was where we tore down walls and painted the remaining ones green, beige, blue, and a combination of red, brown, and golden-yellow. Kevin crawled and took his first steps on the uneven and splintered floor. His boyhood memories were made there. The Vermin served as the backdrop for most of our home videos. Despite its flaws, living there had somehow enhanced our lives. But the time had come to say goodbye.

In February 2012, on our last night in The Vermin, we sat on the sofa in the hollowed-out living room, surrounded by stacked boxes containing our belongings. We took turns reading the letters we had written about our time living there. Kevin's letter summed it up best: "To me," he wrote, "this is the only house I've known. Moving is not easy. I don't remember it, but this is where I met the family that I've come to know and love. The miraculous decision that Judge Cooper made decided our future. She made us the family that we are today. This was our home from December 22, 2000, to February 7, 2012. We shared our lives in this apartment. So as we move forward, I promise to move forward together as a family. I will carry all the experiences I've had here. As you've both said, 'We may leave this apartment, but we will always take our memories with us.' We have to make a decision for the better. One thing I will remember is that wherever my family is, wherever the heart is, I am always home."

The next day, Kevin left for school before the movers arrived. He now walked to and from school on his own. After school, he would come to our new home.

The move itself was straightforward. We didn't have much to transport, and it only took ninety minutes from loading to unloading—the benefits of living in a small space. It also helped that we left larger items like the sofa, dressers, and desk behind for the next tenant.

Around 11 am, my parents showed up unexpectedly and without notice to help us unpack. Although I had told them earlier in the week that we didn't need their help, I'm glad they didn't listen. Mom and Dad were a lifesaver. Mom cleaned and organized our kitchen while Dad took care of the bathroom. This allowed Danny and me to focus on the bedrooms. I reassembled the loft bed and hung Kevin's David Wright poster in his new room.

"So?" Mom asked during our lunch break.

"So what?" I asked in reply.

"Now that you've moved, is there anything else you guys want to do?"

I looked at Danny. We both knew she was referring to marriage.

"We'll have time to discuss other things once we finish unpacking and settling in."

"Okay, but..."

"We'll figure it out."

Many of our friends got married when the law was enacted the previous July. Most of them couldn't understand why, despite being in a committed relationship for fourteen years and raising a child together, I still hesitated. I tried to explain that we already lived like a married couple and didn't require anyone's, especially the government's, stamp of approval.

A few weeks later, our friend Matt tried to convince me otherwise at a Mexican restaurant on Staten Island. "You're being ridiculous," he said. "I didn't fight for your rights, Kevin's rights, in the Assembly for you not to take advantage of those rights. Think about this guy right here." Matt shook Kevin's shoulder to emphasize his point. "The second you get married, you'll immediately gain over a thousand rights and protections for him and your family. If nothing else, do it for him."

"I'll think about it," I said. "I mean, we'll probably do it. It's just a matter of when."

With same-sex marriage dominating the headlines almost every day, the topic was unavoidable. The pressure for Danny and me to tie the knot only grew stronger.

But I still had reservations.

And not at a chapel.

PRE-CANA

My sister and mother itched for us to get married so they could plan our wedding reception. One Saturday evening, they cornered us in a booth at a restaurant in my hometown.

"So, have you thought any more about getting married?" Linda asked, taking a sip of her drink.

"If we do it," I said, "we'll let you know."

"Let us know?" Mom sniped.

"Yeah," I said. "It ain't going to be a big thing if it happens. We'll just go to City Hall, get the paper, and be done with it."

"Oh, come on," Mom said. "Don't be such a party pooper."

"We'll take care of all the planning," Linda said.

"Plus, you'll get gifts," Mom added.

"No gifts," I quickly responded. "I don't want some big gay Italian wedding. Thanks, but no thanks."

"What's wrong with that?" Mom asked.

I had been to enough of those types of gaudy affairs, each trying to outdo the other, and there was no way on earth I'd go along with something even remotely resembling a catering hall extravaganza. A raised dais and raucous DJ? Not on my watch.

"I promise it won't be like that," Linda assured me.

"I don't understand. What's wrong with a big wedding?" Mom asked.

"Nothing," I said. "If that's what the couple wants, it's fine. But it's not what we want."

"I'm excited that my son can finally get married," Mom said as if she were a little girl marrying her Ken dolls. "It'll be fun. You'll get gifts."

"Enough with the gifts," I said. "We're already married. Not legally, but we've been together for fifteen years. There's no need for a circus."

I knew my mom felt cheated. Of her four children, only two had gotten married, and now that I could, she wanted a third grand celebration. Knowing she wouldn't get anywhere with me, she tactically shifted her attention to her golden boy from Texas, hoping to officially make him her son-in-law.

"Is that what you want, Danny?" she asked.

"I'm with Pete," Danny said.

"See," I said, "we're in complete agreement."

Mom feigned dejection and pouted, pretending to be wounded.

"Look, Ma," I softened my tone. "I know you want to be involved and plan a wedding. But if I let you do that, our wedding, if we have one, will no longer be about us and what we want."

"I know, I know," she said, then pivoted to Kevin, who had been listening from the corner. "Don't you think your Papa and Daddy should have a big reception?"

"I don't know," he said. "I guess."

"See," Mom turned to me, "even your son wants you to have a reception." She playfully stuck her tongue out at me.

"Grandma?" Kevin asked. "What's a reception?"

"It's a big, expensive party," I interjected before she could answer. "You're on display all day, people don't leave you alone, and you're forced to perform and do things you don't want to do."

"Oh," Kevin thought for a second, "I don't want to do that."

"Thank you, my son," I said. "We have raised you well."

"I…" Mom began to say something else, but Dad interrupted her.

"All right, enough already, Louise," he said. "Let them do what they want. Geez!"

"For the record," Linda said, smiling at Danny, "I can't wait for you to officially become my favorite brother-in-law."

"He'd be your only brother-in-law," I pointed out.

"I know. I'll get another brother." She smirked sarcastically. "A good one."

"Very funny," I said. "And if anyone thinks about surprising us, I will turn around and walk out. I'm serious, I will. Ask Danny how I reacted when he tried to surprise me on my birthday last year."

"Pete doesn't like surprises," Danny confirmed.

"Why? Surprises are fun," Mom said.

"Okay, that's it," I said, playfully tossing my napkin on the table. "We'll get married. Okay." Danny seemed more surprised than anyone by my sudden announcement. "But no one will know when or where it happens. We won't share the date, time, or place."

"Will you tell me?" Kevin asked.

"Yes. As long as you don't tell them."

"Okay," he agreed, and we fist-bumped.

For the time being, that ended all the talk about us getting married.

To Danny's credit, ever since my rejection in New Hope, he had respected my wish—not to ask that question again—and had not even dropped the slightest hints about anything related to us getting married. I knew if Danny and I were to wed, it would be up to me to propose.

Later that week, after Kevin had gone to bed, while Danny and I sat on the sofa and mindlessly channel surfed, I casually tossed out the idea of us getting married, a trial balloon with barely enough helium.

"My mother and sister are probably right," I said. "We should do it."

"Do what?" he asked.

"Don't be coy. You know what I'm talking about."

"I do?"

"You're not going to make this easy, are you? Can we just agree to get married? Neither one of us has to ask the other."

"That's totally up to you," he said.

"Fine, I get it," I said. "You're forbidden from asking me, and I'm not going to ask you, so let's just say we'll get married."

He shrugged. I took it as a yes.

"Okay, it's settled then."

And there you have it—the least romantic, most cowardly, non-proposal marriage proposal ever.

May 7, 2012

I shared the news with Kevin the next day as we walked to school together. At nearly twelve years old, he was big enough to wear my old T-shirts. Most were threadbare and a tad large, but he loved their worn-in softness. That morning, he wore my favorite Tampa Bay Buccaneers T-shirt. I remembered the day I bought it in the late '80s. That shirt went everywhere with me. I wore it under softball jerseys and bowling shirts. I wore it to the gym because it made my arms look bigger. It had been all mine for over twenty years, but now it belonged to Kevin.

I should have known it would become his. He had marked it with drool on the first day he came home.

I looked down at my feet. While he wore my old shirt, I had inherited his barely used sneakers. We shared the same shoe size for a brief time. His feet grew so fast, he needed a larger size every other month. As a result, all his size 9-1/2s became mine.

"So, your dad and I are going to get married," I said matter-of-factly.

"That's cool," he said.

"We haven't figured out the details yet, but…"

"Don't judges marry people?" Kevin interrupted. He had apparently given it some thought. "Why don't you ask the judge who did my adoption to do your wedding?"

"Hmm," I said. "That's a great idea." I sensed there was more to his suggestion. "Would you like to meet her?"

"Sure. Think she'd remember me?"

"There's only one way to find out."

When I got back home, I composed a query letter and sent it to the email address of Manhattan Family Court that I found online:

> I'm writing to find out how to get in contact with Judge Cooper. My partner and I would like to ask her if she would preside over our marriage this summer.
>
> Judge Cooper created our family over 10 years ago when she placed our son—at the time an abandoned infant who was found on the subway by my partner, Danny—in our home and then presided over the final adoption. We would be honored if she would also preside over our upcoming marriage. We don't know how to get in contact with her, hence this email.
>
> If you could put me in contact with the appropriate person in Judge Cooper's chambers or inform me of the proper procedures to make such a request, it would be greatly appreciated.

Two hours later, I received a response from a court attorney:

> I am the court attorney to Judge Cooper. I received your email regarding your request to have Judge Cooper perform your marriage ceremony. I spoke to the judge, and she was very delighted and is extremely interested.

I called the court attorney immediately. We spoke about the process and possible dates. I asked if July 13th was available. She said she'd check with the judge and get back to me. The next day, I received this email:

> The judge would like to meet privately with the two of you on Monday, June 4, 2012, for a twenty-minute interview. Please do not bring any others with you. Also, the judge stated that she is available Friday, July 13, 2012, for the ceremony.

There was no turning back. The time had come to protect our family and legalize our de facto marriage.

June 4, 2012

We hadn't been to the Family Court Building since Kevin's adoption. Plus, when we had gone, all our interactions were from a distance, separated by tables, lawyers, caseworkers, stenographers, and the judge's bench. Now, it would just be the three of us, face-to-face, in a more intimate setting.

The judge's court attorney met us in the lobby and escorted us to the judge's office, where Judge Cooper stood just inside the doorway. Initially, we felt unsure about the protocol for entering a judge's office and awkwardly waited outside for a few seconds. However, Judge Cooper quickly put us at ease with her warm smile and handshake. She expressed happiness about officiating our wedding and gestured for us to enter her office by leaning against the door to open it further.

"Have a seat," she said, pointing to the sofa across from her desk.

Outside the courtroom and away from the bench, Judge Cooper appeared shorter, down-to-earth and spoke more softly than we had remembered. Her office decor matched her demeanor. Warm colors mixed with wood and leather—a cozy room that invited you in for a cup of tea, but also a somber place where the fates of children and families were considered and determined. Everything had a comfortable worn-in feel as if the furnishings hadn't changed in thirty years, giving it the atmosphere of a sepia-toned, matte-finished photograph.

As she closed the door, Judge Cooper asked, "Do you want me to wear my robe?" Her robe hung on a hook behind the door. "The last wedding I performed, the couple wanted me to wear it."

"No, it's not necessary," I replied, glancing nervously at Danny. The idea of getting married by a judge in a robe felt too formal for our taste. For all we cared, Judge Cooper could wear a muumuu if she wanted—whatever made her comfortable.

"I'll wear it if you want me to," she said.

"That's okay," Danny said.

"Good," she said with a sigh of relief.

Judge Cooper seemed more reserved than we remembered. There was no trace of her stern courtroom demeanor. She carefully chose her words, taking pauses before speaking. It was apparent that her thirty years as a family court judge had taught her to avoid displaying emotions or becoming too personally invested. We suspected that maintaining professional detachment was necessary for her to apply the law fairly and impartially. She was a mystery, and that intimidated us.

Pulling up a chair, Judge Cooper immediately inquired about Kevin. She wanted to know how he was doing in school, what his interests were, and how he had been since she last saw him. We informed her that Kevin was a hardworking, kind, conscientious student. We updated her on his interests over the past ten years, which included baseball, magic, juggling, swimming, ultimate frisbee, and his latest passion, dancing with the National Dance Institute (NDI).

By then, Kevin had been dancing with NDI for four years. He had received an invitation and scholarship to join the troupe. Kevin had rehearsals every night the following week for NDI's big year-end event, *Inner Visions: A Celebration of Stevie Wonder*. He was set to be featured in a salsa/ballroom dance performance to the song "Don't You Worry 'Bout a Thing." The title and choreography perfectly matched Kevin's smooth and easy-going personality.

When Danny and I reflected on how Kevin's life began and how far he had come, from being alone in a cold and isolated subway corner to performing in front of a warm and loving jam-packed theater, our emotions were impossible to hold back. Our once scared and guarded infant had blossomed into a confident, intrepid, and footloose young man who was carefree and didn't worry about a thing.

Two proud parents, we effusively touted and rambled on about Kevin's talents and accomplishments. She was impressed with his discipline and devotion.

"I'm looking forward to meeting him," she said but admitted feeling nervous. She rarely saw the long-term results of a placement decision. What if Kevin was unhappy and wished he had different parents?

"To ease your mind," I said, "it was Kevin's idea to ask you to perform our wedding. He can't wait to meet you."

"We're all incredibly grateful you made us a family," Danny said.

Judge Cooper balked at Danny's comment. She refused to take credit and deflected, stating she was just doing her job.

Speaking of her job, Danny and I still had questions, nagging questions that we had asked ourselves on and off for ten years:

What led her to have a hunch?

How was she able to place Kevin with us so quickly?

Did she bend the rules to make us a family?

Up until that point, we could only speculate. However, with her right in front of us, we had to ask.

She decided to answer the last question first.

No, she didn't bend the rules. She explained that during the time our case moved through the system, there was a pilot project in place to prioritize permanency for foster children, especially in situations of abandonment. The program's goal was to move infants without biological attachments into permanent homes as soon as possible so they wouldn't languish in foster care for years. In other words, they intervened early to prevent a child from getting lost in the system, which almost happened to Kevin with his initial placement. The program granted Judge Cooper the authority to expedite procedures and accelerate cases as she saw fit. From her perspective, the foster care agency and ACS had failed Kevin. Therefore, as soon as she became aware of the neglectful conditions in his first foster home, she wasted no time using her authority.

Unfortunately, as Judge Cooper lamented, the pilot project was discontinued shortly after our adoption. She didn't elaborate on the reasons but hinted that the program lacked sufficient funding and resources.

"That's a real shame," I said. It broke our hearts to think about all the kids who ended up back in the slow lane, possibly never finding a forever family. We considered ourselves lucky. The timing had been perfect. The window of opportunity had been open just long enough for us to pass through. We knew luck played a big part in becoming a family but learning about the pilot program added another layer of amazement. Without knowing it, we were in the right place at the right time to benefit from a short-lived, fast-track program with a judge dedicated to her job.

As we marveled at the unbelievable synchronicity, Judge Cooper surprised us with another miracle of timing. "I'm retiring this November," she said. "If you had waited any longer, I might not have been here to marry you." Officiating our wedding and seeing Kevin, she said, would be a wonderful way to bring her thirty years on the bench to a close.

As for her "hunch," Judge Cooper sighed as if to ask, how does one explain a hunch?

"Was it something you read about Danny in the police report?" I asked.

"No."

"Did you think he'd make a good parent because he was a social worker?"

"No."

"Did you know he was gay?"

"No." She paused, reflected, and then looked at Danny. "The only person this baby had a connection to was you. You bonded with him that night in a way no one else could."

Her decision to ask Danny to adopt hadn't been premeditated. She made it in the spur of the moment during his testimony. She trusted her instincts. While she accounted for Baby Ace's basic needs—food, shelter, clothing—the judge seemed to base her hunch on his emotional needs, the fundamental need to belong and be loved. After hearing Danny's testimony, she concluded he and Baby Ace belonged together.

For the past decade, we had mythologized her as a wand-waving, grant-wishing fairy godmother. The truth was less romantic and more pragmatic. For starters, she used a gavel, not a magic wand. And as for our sexual orientation, it was irrelevant to her. Judge Cooper made it clear she wasn't trying to make any political statement by allowing us, two gay men, to become a family.

Our twenty-minute visit doubled.

At forty-five minutes, Judge Cooper retrieved a manila folder from her desk. Inside was a 2003 letter and photo of

Kevin from my mom. I had no idea Mom had sent the letter and photo. (Yet one more revelation.)

We read the letter:

Dear Judge Cooper:

Enclosed is a photo of my grandson, Kevin. Last December, you approved his adoption to Danny and my son Peter. Kevin is now three years old and is a thriving, happy, and very bright child. He has given our entire family such joy and love. We cannot visualize life without him. He is our "Special K."

He loves when his aunts and uncles and cousins are together for birthdays, celebrations and holidays. He communicates so well and loves to have conversations, especially with Grandma (me). We talk about everything. Kevin loves to read, play bug bingo, go to the movies, Sesame Street, Crayola Factory, and see shows. He sings and dances. He has become a well-rounded little boy. He loves to play T-Ball and golf. He just started swimming lessons at the YMCA. His favorite thing to do is play with trains and go on the subway with his Daddy and Papa. When the moment is right, his fathers will tell him how he was found. For now, he is just content to be loved and cared for. Danny and Peter are wonderful parents.

I just thought it would be nice to let you know Kevin's progress. So many times, we take things for granted and forget to say thank you for our blessings.

On behalf of my family, we wish to thank you for seeing something in Danny and Peter to grant them the privilege of making Kevin part of our family.

Best Regards,
Louise (alias Grandma)

Judge Cooper carefully returned the letter and photo to the folder, a keepsake from a grateful grandma, and placed them on her desk for safekeeping. Then, she refocused her attention on the matter at hand.

"Will you be exchanging rings?" she asked.

"No," I responded.

To me, a ring was nothing more than a finger noose. The thought of my finger swelling and strangling an important digit distressed me greatly. How would I ever type an s, w, or x if I lost my ring finger?

Judge Cooper frowned, bypassed me, and looked directly at Danny, using a tactic my mom often employed.

"We'll exchange something else," I offered. "Another symbol of our love and commitment. Maybe a pendant."

Judge Cooper looked puzzled. I could tell she was envisioning the ceremony without rings. How would the part where you say, "With this ring I thee wed" be replaced? Would it become "With this medallion I thee wed?"

"I think you should reconsider rings," she politely advised.

"We'll think about it," I said. Oh, we almost forgot. We have something for you." I reached into my bag and pulled out a copy of *The Boy from New York City*. A few weeks earlier, I had created three hardcover versions of the book using an online service—one for ourselves, one for my mom, and one for Judge Cooper.

"We made this for Kevin when he was little," Danny explained.

Judge Cooper quickly flipped through the pages and smiled when she saw her character.

"I like how I turned out," she commented.

"Oh good," I said, "I was afraid you wouldn't."

"No, I look good."

"This is for you to keep," Danny said.

Judge Cooper closed the book and held it close to her chest with both arms. "I will cherish this forever," she expressed.

The meeting had surpassed an hour. It was time to leave. We stood up and thanked Judge Cooper once more. "We will see you on July 13th."

Once we were outside, I had a change of heart about the rings. I realized that getting married and exchanging rings didn't mean that I would lose a finger. In fact, the image of two circles coming together as one symbolized a powerful representation of our love and commitment.

"Let's get rings," I said.

Danny smiled. He had also wanted rings but didn't want to push his luck. The most important thing for him was that we were finally getting married.

Over the next week, we dedicated our evenings to sorting out the details of the ceremony and the party. We decided to call it a party instead of a reception to keep the vibe within our comfort zone: informal and low-key. Neither of us enjoyed big, fancy affairs, stuffy events, or pretentious gatherings. We contacted our friends at Cowgirl and reserved their kitschy western lounge area and back dining room for Sunday, July 15th.

The next day, I designed the invitations.

CELEBRATE

PETE & DANNY

ARE GETTING MARRIED

PLEASE COME PARTY WITH US

SUNDAY, JULY 15, 2012 4–6PM
BAR K @ COWGIRL
NEW YORK CITY

— DRINKS, FOOD, FESTIVITIES —

{ it's casual, yee-haw }

Our party, our way, would be far less dress-up and much more hoe-down. And since we were regulars at Cowgirl, it would feel like everyone was coming to our home.

"Do you want to invite your parents to the ceremony?" I asked Danny one night as we went through the guest list.

"I doubt they'd come," he said.

"How about the party?"

"I don't know."

Although Danny's mom had made some progress in accepting our relationship and acknowledging our parenting skills, he still didn't believe she or any other family member would attend or participate in our celebration. Yet, he wanted to avoid making assumptions. So the next day, he called his mom to share the news.

"When I told her we were getting married," Danny recounted, "she didn't say anything."

"Nothing at all?"

"No, nothing. So we moved on to other topics."

Two weeks later, Danny received a letter from his mom.

In the letter, she expressed her unconditional love for him, emphasizing it with underlined words. However, she went on to explain that because "God says homosexuality is an abomination to Him," she and his dad did "not approve of the union of homosexuals."

Although Danny anticipated a response like this, the letter still hurt him.

"To know my parents choose not to share in my happiness and choose not to celebrate a joyous occasion that honors and strengthens my commitment to my partner of fifteen years, one that protects the family we've created, makes me incredibly sad. As a parent, I could never imagine not sharing in my son's joy and happiness. Unconditional love is unwavering. She always says that God has a plan for all of us. I wish she could see and accept that my family and the love I share with you and Kevin are a part of that plan."

Danny wrote a lengthy response expressing disappointment and sadness. He challenged his mom's biblical interpretations:

> You believe all things are possible through Jesus Christ. It is my sincere hope that through Jesus, your heart and mind can be changed, and you can come to a new acceptance. I choose to surround myself with people in my life who love and support me and accept me for who I am—because I am gay—not despite it. Unconditional love is unwavering. It is complete and whole and selfless. I hope that you can accept me for who I am and love me unconditionally. I hope you can open your heart and mind and come to a new understanding.

"I refuse to dwell or fester in anger over this," he added, folding the letter and placing it in an envelope.

Throughout our fifteen years together, there were many moments when I wished Danny would have allowed me to see this kind of hurt so I could have comforted him, as he often comforted me. Still waters run deep with him.

"I could never fathom anything, anyone, any belief, or any ideology coming between us and Kevin," I declared. "Allowing that to happen is beyond my comprehension. That's the true abomination. I can't believe it took me fifteen years to say yes to marrying you. I'm a schmuck."

I hugged him tightly.

THERE

July 13, 2012

Our big day. The second biggest day in our lives. And we still didn't have rings. No, I didn't flip-flop. We didn't want to spend a lot of money on them, so we ordered cheap titanium bands on Amazon. It turned out to be a good decision because Danny has lost his ring three times since then. So, going inexpensive was the right choice, although maybe we should've splurged for faster delivery.

The morning felt familiar, reminiscent of the morning of our adoption ten years earlier, except now Kevin dressed himself. He stood before the mirror, adjusting and readjusting his new tie.

"Need any help?" Danny asked.

"No." After watching Kevin make several unsuccessful attempts at getting the knot and length just right, I finally asked if he wanted my assistance.

"No, I got it," he replied, frustrated and annoyed. He wouldn't admit it, but he had a case of the jitters percolating under his cool veneer. Kevin untied the knot, removed the tie, draped it around his neck again, checked the side lengths, and started over. I thought it had looked fine several tries ago, but he aimed for perfection.

Danny and I opted to wear khakis and navy sports coats. In keeping with the tradition of having something old, something new, something borrowed, and something blue on your wedding day, the sports coats fulfilled the "something blue" requirement. If it were solely up to me, we would've married in vintage T-shirts and blue jeans.

Since we didn't have rings, Danny and I scurried around the apartment, trying to find something symbolic to exchange. We rummaged through a shoebox filled with random items and unearthed two tarnished rings from Danny's college days. He slid one onto his finger. It still fit perfectly. "Try this," he said, handing the other ring to me. It barely made it past the tip of my pinky finger.

"What else can we use?" I asked.

"Nothing. These will do for today," he replied. So, we had something old and something borrowed. Now, all we needed was something new, and it was right in front of us: Kevin's tie.

"Looks great," I complimented our boy as he checked himself in the mirror. His effort paid off. As his grandma would say, "You look handsome and spiffy."

We gave Kevin the tarnished proxy rings. He stuffed them into his pocket, and we set off. Just as we left the building, the mail carrier entered—yet another manifestation of exquisite timing. Our mail usually arrived late in the afternoon or sometimes even early in the evening, but today, she was three hours early.

"Do you have anything for 9B?" I asked. She searched the cart's side pouches and pulled out a padded envelope. I glanced at the return address. It was our rings, arriving just in the nick of time.

"We're going to be late," I said, handing the envelope to Kevin. "Let's open it on the way."

It was muggy, soupy, and downright oppressive outside. Within seconds, the humidity shrink-wrapped our clothes onto our bodies. We had planned to take the subway, but we knew it would be like a furnace underground. We'd be drenched in sweat by the time we reached the courthouse. So, I hailed a cab.

During the ride downtown, Kevin tore open the package containing the rings. He carefully examined and compared their sizes. He put his dad's smaller ring in his left pocket and his papa's larger ring in his right for safekeeping. Despite the weather, Danny remained calm and cool, as usual. I was calm, too, but my pulse fluttered. We didn't say much during the ten-minute cab ride. When we got out of the taxi, we paused briefly to take in the metal lettering on the building that read "New York County Family Court" before entering.

Even though there was no line at security, we still followed the snaking tension straps. We placed our belongings on the conveyor belt and passed through the metal detectors without issues. "Don't forget the rings," Danny reminded Kevin from the other side.

"I've got them," Kevin assured us.

Once we gathered our belongings, we went to the elevator bank. When we arrived at our floor and stepped out, a security guard remarked, "We don't get many happy occasions like this around here." He then escorted us to the waiting area. As we turned the corner, we spotted my parents. Mom held a small bouquet of balloons. On a nearby table were brownies, a cupcake tower, and champagne bottles.

"Hey, K-man!" my dad greeted Kevin. Despite once warning us about how a baby would affect the rest of our lives, Dad was always thrilled to see his grandson.

"Look at you," Mom said. "So handsome and spiffy."

"Hi, Grandma," Kevin cheerfully greeted her.

"Where's my hug?" she playfully asked, and Kevin leaned in for a hug.

"This is a big day," Dad observed. "Are you ready?" Kevin nodded and smiled confidently. He was ready for his dads to marry and even more ready to meet Judge Cooper. "Look at all this stuff," Dad continued, transitioning from one thought to another. "I told your grandmother to keep it simple, but she couldn't help herself. She even baked a cake and—"

"But I have nothing to cut it with," Mom finished his sentence and laughed.

"She tried sneaking in a knife, but it set off the metal detectors downstairs, and she got caught red-handed. Your grandmother's a criminal," Dad exclaimed jokingly as he playfully nudged Kevin.

"Oh, Sam, stop," Mom said. "I forgot I had it in my pocketbook. I'll get it back when we leave."

The lighthearted banter between my parents provided some distraction and made the wait feel a bit shorter. However, the cheerful mood quickly faded when Mom pulled out two black baseball caps embroidered with the word "Groom" from her bag.

"Oh, dear lord," I murmured to Danny, "she's going to make us wear those."

"These are for you," Mom said, handing one to Danny and me. "Put them on." She raised her camera. "Stand in front of the balloons."

Danny stifled a laugh as he placed the cap on his head. "One picture," he said, motioning for me to put mine on.

"I got these for you guys to wear at the party. Smile." We posed, and she snapped a few pictures. The caps reminded me of the customized "#1 Papa" and "#1 Daddy" T-shirts she gave us for our first Father's Day in 2001. While we wore those shirts just once, we've kept them forever. I imagined the same would happen with the "Groom" caps. I must give it up to my mom; the caps were the perfect gift. Since I had worn a baseball cap almost every day for the last twenty years, I felt naked without one. Wearing it made me feel less exposed and calmed my nerves a little.

Mom was downright giddy. She had never imagined a day when her son could marry the man he loved. None of us had. I left the cap on, proud to wear it and announce the momentous truth.

A few minutes later, my brother Matt, Linda, and her five-year-old daughter, Madeline, arrived. Madeline ran straight over to Kevin and latched onto his leg. She idolized him. And while usually uncomfortable with the attention and pedestal his younger cousin put him on—he often shooed her away—he made an exception that day and hugged her back.

Our friends Joe, Maya, and Kate showed up a few minutes later.

"Let me know when you're all here," said the security guard.

"This is it," I said. "This is everybody."

"Okay then, follow me," he said.

Our entourage walked down the hall to Judge Cooper's office.

Here we go. We're about to get married. Kevin is about to meet Judge Cooper.

I placed my hand on Kevin's shoulder. In return, he flashed me the warmest smile I had ever seen.

The judge watched us approach, standing just inside her office door like she had for Danny and me a month earlier. Danny and I introduced our family and friends one by one, saving the best for last. Judge Cooper's face lit up when she saw

Kevin. Everyone else turned to watch them greet each other. Kevin extended his arm for a handshake.

"Can I give you a hug?" Judge Cooper asked. Kevin, a few inches taller, bent down and hugged her. Then, he stood still for a moment, feeling awkward and unsure what to say or do next.

"Come in, come in." The judge gestured for all of us to enter her office. Once we were all inside, Judge Cooper closed the door. "Sit, sit," she said.

Mom, Dad, Linda, and Madeline sat on the sofa. Our friends stood around the edges. After a few minutes of chit-chat and small talk, the judge reminded us of the purpose for being there and asked, "Shall we begin?"

Danny and I moved into position next to Kevin, who held the rings in his pockets. Judge Cooper picked up the boilerplate script we had discussed during our previous visit, but it didn't include the vows we had written for each other.

"Um," I said. "We didn't go over this in June, but we wrote vows. Would it be okay if we read them first?"

"Of course," she replied.

"You go first," Danny said.

I unfolded the paper in my pocket. The vows trembled in my hand. The weight of what we were about to do choked me up, and I couldn't find my voice. I glanced at Danny and then at Kevin, tears streaming down my face. Kevin placed a comforting hand on my back to calm my nerves.

I took a deep breath.

"First, before I begin," I said directly to Danny, "I need to retract a response I gave you over fourteen years ago and change my answer to 'Yes.' Now, when we decided to get married and started sharing the news with others, I've offered caveats like, 'Well, it's really just a formality of what already is,' or 'We're doing it for our son, for our family,' or 'Because of all the legal rights we'll get.' And while those are all acceptable answers, the only answer that matters is that I love you. You are a gentle, loving, devoted, honest, patient, and caring soul and an affectionate and attentive companion. There are so many things that make you uniquely you. Allow me to point out a few. Your pleased-with-yourself cheesy smile. The way you stick your tongue out when you concentrate. Your corny-themed music playlists. Your part-cadaver knee that also serves as a barometer. Your spontaneous whistling, which, for better or worse, Kevin has now inherited. I love that you're a romantic and not a cynic. I love that you still want to surprise me. Yes, deep down, I do love that you want to surprise me. And so, starting today, the ban on surprises has been lifted. And even though I joke that your bright, rust-colored corduroys are a definite deal-breaker, I love them. They are you, rusty and with ridges, but also immensely soft and timeless. And most important, your awareness and heroic actions on a fateful August evening eleven years ago that changed both of our lives forever. You're a terrific father. I'm proud of you. I'm proud of us. I look forward to growing old with you. Well, older. Since we're already more than halfway there. There's still so much life for us to explore and discover together. Let's keep dreaming. Let's keep believing in miracles. Let's do this thing."

Now it was Danny's turn.

"Okay, give me a second," he said to Judge Cooper and everyone else, wiping away tears. "I didn't expect to cry." He looked down at his notes, drew a deep breath, and began.

"Pete, our lives have been a journey marked by the bending of fate. Who would have thought a transported Texan would meet and fall for a New Jersey Italian? We came from different worlds and found each other. I knew shortly after we met you were the one I had been looking for. You asked me 'How can you be so sure?' I had a hunch, was I wrong?" Danny glanced at Judge Cooper to see if she recognized the reference, then continued. "I remember shortly after we met, I asked 'Will you still love me when I'm all gray?' You responded, 'Will you still love me when I'm bald?' Well, both of those things happened too quickly! I love your wit and sense of humor. I love your playfulness, even when you annoy me. I am drawn to your strength and vulnerability. You have a gentle and caring heart—often masked in sarcasm—yet radiates throughout and melts my heart when I feel the love you give me. I love that you put up with my incessant whistling. Our life together has been a journey and I want to be by your side as we continue on this journey. Although I may not be good with directions, and I get lost easily, I know you are right there to help me get back on the right path, or as you like to say, 'You're other right!' I can't promise to always know where I'm going, but together, we will eventually get there."

There.

We weren't supposed to be there—two men with a son we had never dreamed of by our side, getting married by a woman who changed and enriched our lives more than she would ever know. But there we were, thanks to a fateful discovery and a judicious hunch.

Sometimes the getting there felt like a dream. As if I had fallen asleep at 7:45 pm on August 28, 2000, and never woke up. It is the sweetest, most vivid, and beautiful dream. In it, there is a baby, a boy, who became our son. But Danny and I didn't have a son. And yet, the dream felt incredibly real, especially when I held our boy tight and rubbed his back or when I tickled his belly and he laughed uncontrollably. We taught this boy how to walk, talk, wipe his booty, brush his teeth, tie his shoes, and ride a bike. We laughed, and we danced and monkey-hugged every chance we got. Danny and I showed our son the world, and he expanded ours. The dream was filled with so much warmth, happiness, fulfillment, and, most importantly, unconditional love. But at 7:45 pm on August 28, 2000, I didn't have definitions for happiness, fulfillment, or love. So that meant what I had envisioned must have been only a dream.

In real time, back in the judge's office, I took Danny's hand in mine. Our fingers intertwined and became one. We surveyed our loved ones' faces. My mom, sister, and niece wiped away tears of joy. My dad and brother nodded approvingly. Our friends held their hands over their hearts. Judge Cooper, the woman who made all of this possible, smiled.

We looked back at Kevin, the glue in our relationship. Without him, we wouldn't be a family. Our best man, he held our rings in the palms of his hands. We were fixated on his broad, flawless smile. There he was, the boy in a dream we never dreamt but which came true anyway. He was the reason we were all there, our daily reminder that anything is possible.

Our miracle.

Our fate.

Our forever.

He was surrounded by love and beamed like the happiest kid in the world.

ACKNOWLEDGMENTS

A big heartfelt thank you to:

Everyone who was there in the beginning and helped us become a family: case workers at both foster care and adoption agencies, including Gail, Joyce, Karey, Elizabeth, Marshall, Sharhonda, Noemi, Stephen, Margaret; the Administration for Children's Services and Legal Aid representatives, Karen, Terri, Jill, Theresa, and Rhoda; and everyone at Manhattan Family Court, especially Judge Cooper.

The village of friends who helped us raise our son and for being available on a moment's notice to babysit for, look after or hang out with him: Chuck Blasius, Joe Hosking, Dean Taylor, Roger Anderson, Brandon Berry, Oscar Lopolito, Mark Lilakos, Ricky Lizalde, Sheilah James, Sarah Donovan, Melanie Bean, Reggie Brown, Martha Towler, John Motondo, Anna Wheatley, Michael Liguori, Frank Haupt, Phil Jimenez, Josh Pugliese, Matthew Titone, Mason Scherzer, Scott Heim, Michael Lowenthal, Steve Bowman, Rich Stanton, Scott Keeney, Frank Graves, Priscilla Lang, Desi Joseph, Mindy Raymond Benson, Jennifer Skinner, William Wagner, Bill Bigelow, Bruce Beckwith, Henri Simonetti, Maryann Kenney, Peggy Rey, Katy Whelan, Charlie Edwards, all the coworkers who allowed Kevin to nap and play in their offices, and all the folks at Cowgirl for always making us feel special.

Kevin's mentors—the teachers, counselors, coaches, music and dance instructors who inspired all of us: Pam, Eddie, Brian, Michele, Kelly, Meg, Brooke, and a special shout-out to everyone at National Dance Institute. It's true—the arts do have the power to engage children and motivate them toward excellence.

Dr. Macek, Alexandra, and Lana for keeping Kevin healthy. Marcus Lazzaro for helping to keep me sane and honest.

Our families: Mom and Dad (Sam and Louise Mercurio), Linda, Matthew, Joseph, Lisa, Daniel, Christian, Madeline, Danny's parents, brothers, sisters, cousins, nephews, and nieces in Texas and beyond.

For their guidance: Stuart Krichevsky, Laura Usselman, Cathy Saypol, Ross Harris, Allen Zadoff, Michele Farinet, Michael Denneny.

For my dear boys, Danny and Kevin, for showing me how to love and be loved and making me a better human. I hope I've done our story justice and made you proud. And finally, Nagano! (Danny and Kevin know what that means, and that's all that matters.)

ABOUT THE AUTHOR

Peter Mercurio is a writer, husband, and dad. He enjoys hiking and exploring the National Parks, cycling, kayaking, with his husband and son.

Other works:

Children's picture book
Our Subway Baby

Screenplay
Found

Stage plays
Andrew Reaches The Other Side
Two Spoons
Hatch
Red and Tan Line

For more by Pete, please visit petermercurio.com

SNAPSHOTS

SNAPSHOTS 239

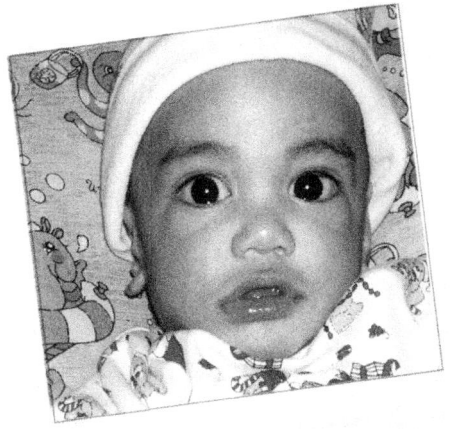

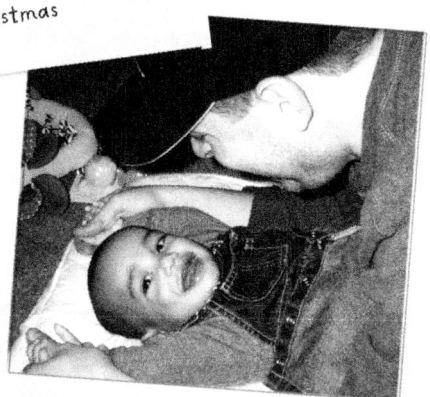

First Christmas

Papa stretching my arms

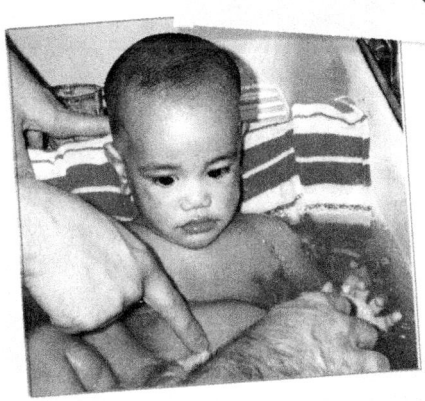

Grandma's sink bath

Learning to crawl

At a Rookies game

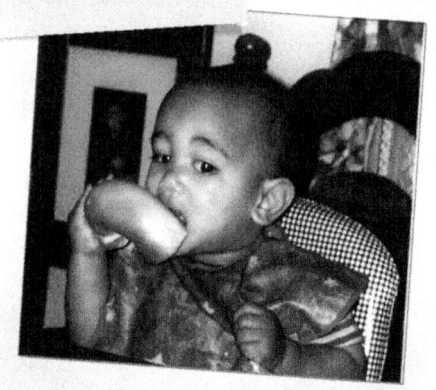

Yummy bagel

SNAPSHOTS 241

Papa and me

Daddy and me on the subway

Riding a tractor in Texas

With Daddy along the Hudson River

With Papa along the Hudson River

Wearing stripes

First day of kindergarten

Little league

Papa and Daddy Lovin'

Monkey hug

Dad and me in Coney Island

NYC skyline

Brooklyn Bridge

Catching air

Getting wet

Grand Canyon

Zion National Park

Let's Go Mets!

SNAPSHOTS 247

Leaping with NDI

Grooms

The day my dads got married

See ya

Thank you.

Printed in Dunstable, United Kingdom